All the material in this book has been devised and run in a variety of venues by the author, John Hardwick. John works under the banner of *Counties* and *Children Worldwide* to present the Christian message in an exciting way that will appeal to people of all ages. Equally well received in schools, churches and at outreach events, John's skills in clowning, juggling, unicycling, storytelling, music composition and performance are a proven success. He leads *Creative Communications* training events for those involved in children's ministry and all-age services and is a familiar face at Spring Harvest, Easter People and other Christian events, where he leads family and children's sessions. John is a member of the *Barnabas Live* team, author of the popular holiday club resource *We're going on a Jungle Jamboree* and co-author of the Holiday Club section in *Out of the Toybox*, also published by BRF.

Text copyright © John Hardwick 2004
Illustrations copyright © Simon Smith 2004
The author asserts the moral right
to be identified as the author of this work

Published by
The Bible Reading Fellowship
First Floor, Elsfield Hall
15–17 Elsfield Way, Oxford OX2 8FG

ISBN 1 84101 185 1
First published 2004
10 9 8 7 6 5 4 3 2 1 0
All rights reserved

Acknowledgments
Unless otherwise stated, scripture quotations are taken from the Good News Bible
published by The Bible Societies/HarperCollins Publishers Ltd, UK © American Bible
Society 1966, 1971, 1976, 1992, used with permission.
Performance and copyright

The right to perform *Champions!* drama material is included in the purchase price,
so long as the performance is in an amateur context, for instance in church services,
schools or holiday club venues.

Where any charge is made to audiences, written permission must be obtained from
the author, who can be contacted through the publishers. A fee or royalties may be
payable for the right to perform the script in that context.

A catalogue record for this book is available from the British Library

Printed and bound in Malta

Champions!

A five-day holiday club plan, complete and ready-to-run

John Hardwick

*I want to dedicate this book to my father, Leslie Hardwick, and my late mother, Ruth,
who since long before I was born have been involved in reaching out to children,
through Skegness beach mission, camps and regular Sunday school and midweek children's clubs.
They have helped me to see the importance of reaching out to children
who often know nothing about the Bible or of God's love for them.*

Acknowledgments

*My thanks to the following people for their help and inspiration:
John's wife Rachel, and children Chloe and Ben
Colleagues in the work, David Illiffe, Alan Charter, Mel Owen, Michelle Ellwood,
Sue Doggett, Andrea Thompson, Paul Willmott and Steve Whyatt.
With many thanks to David Wilkinson for the sheet music notation
and helping me record the* High-Energy Holiday Club Songs *CD.
Also Simon Smith, for his fantastic artwork.
Thanks also to the people of Hasbury Christian Fellowship,
St Neots Evangelical Church, Easter People, and Cym-Ipswich for allowing me
to try out my new theme on them and for helping with ideas.*

Contents

Introduction

Setting up

Choose sports-related team names from different disciplines, such as 'pole vaulters' and 'shot putters', and appropriate dress for your leaders and assistants. You'll need craft leaders and games leaders to lead champion crafts and champion games, and a team leader to oversee the sessions.

Choose team colours and names to match the theme. To create a sporty atmosphere, decorate your venue to look like a sports arena, with bunting and a selection of national flags. If you have the resources available, you might like to paint a stadium backdrop, showing the Olympic rings and seated areas with the crowds watching the events.

Overview

Champions! introduces us to the life of Jesus and how he 'ran the race' for God. It is designed to encourage children also to run that race, running straight towards the goal and finishing the race in order to win the ultimate prize of taking their place in heaven. This is the prize that God offers each one of us through the work of his Son, Christ Jesus.

All the Bible stories are taken from the life of Jesus and link into the memory verses, which are taken from the New Testament letters. Day One, *Direction*, looks at the story of Jesus in the temple from Luke 2:41–52; Day Two, *Distraction*, uses the story of Jesus' temptations in the desert from Matthew 4:1–11; Day Three, *Dedication*, tells the story of the paralysed man and his four friends from Mark 2:1–12; Day Four, *Determination*, focuses on the events of the cross and resurrection; and Day Five, *Decoration*, celebrates the fact that Jesus is alive and victorious through the story of his ascension.

Roles and responsibilities

Champions! academy staff

Good teamwork is essential for good children's work. As well as an overall holiday club co-ordinator, you'll need people to fill all the following roles.

Registration officer

This role would suit a well-organized person. If the children are registered before the start date of the holiday club, you will save time on the first day of the club. If you choose to register the children on the first day, you will need a good team of helpers to cope with the workload.

You need to register the following details for each child (see form on p. 62):

- Name
- Address
- Date of birth
- Contact phone numbers
- Medical details (such as asthma or allergies)
- Parent's or guardian's permission for child to attend the club

You will need to split children into groups according to their age bands, and possibly sub-section them into teams. It's advisable to issue each child with a colour-coded sticker or badge to identify them and their team (see p. 60). Have a 'welcome' team available 15 minutes before the start, to make the children feel at home when they arrive.

Team 'coaches'

Team leaders (or 'coaches') need to be able to deal with a high level of responsibility. Each team leader will be allocated to a particular group of children or age band. They will stay with the children the whole time, sitting with them and leading them through various activities. They will befriend, enthuse and maintain a level of control. It's important that team leaders join in the songs, as children will look to their leaders as role models.

Team helpers

These are people who can help the team leaders. They need to be free to fetch things, accompany children to the toilet and so on.

Fitness instructor (Games leader)

This needs to be someone with experience of sorting children quickly and of organizing games. A powerful voice would be an asset! Keep the games in one location and bring the children to that area when it is their turn to play.

Craft leader

This needs to be someone able to organize a simple craft activity. The craft leader will need to start collecting materials well in advance. Try to make the crafts related to the theme. Once again, have a fixed location for crafts, and bring the children to that area when it is their turn to participate.

Time keeper

This person keeps an eye on the time and gives a five-minute warning to activity leaders that the session is about to end. The time keeper then rings a bell when it's time for the teams to move on to the next activity.

Dieticians (Snack team)

One person, or team, is needed to prepare drinks and biscuits for the children. Not all the children will need their drinks at the same time, as teams will take turns to have their refreshments. Please ensure that all the leaders, including the games leader and craft leader, also receive drinks.

Physio (First aider)

It is essential to have someone available who is a trained first aider, and to have a well-stocked first aid box. St John Ambulance may be able to offer advice if you are unsure about how to provide this facility.

Response team

Children may have questions about the Christian faith. Members of the response team need to be able to talk in simple language, be good listeners, and know what they believe and how to put it across without manipulation or forcing the children into making statements or promises that they cannot understand or keep.

You will need to think about how to follow up children who are seeking to know more about the Christian faith.

Publicity officer

This person is needed to design and organize posters, leaflets and school visits, and to contact the local press.

Floaters

Floaters are people who cannot commit themselves to attend the whole week's programme but are able to come for a day or two. They can help wherever there is a need.

Trainers (Stage team or Presenter)

Either one person or a team is needed to lead the up-front programme, including leading the songs, theme illustration, quiz, Bible story and teaching, and introducing the drama and puppet sketch. You may wish to fill this role from your own team, or you may decide to give your regular children's leaders a rest and bring in someone from outside. See page 75 for organizations who have presenters available.

Dos and don'ts

It's worth repeating that good children's work relies on good teamwork!

- Do sit in with the children during up-front time.
- Do be prepared to join in songs and interactive parts of the programme. Don't forget that children will look to the team leaders as their role models.
- Do encourage, befriend and control your team of children.
- Do encourage children to go to the toilet during the activities times rather than the up-front/teaching times. Remember that children follow each other's lead: if you're not careful, all the young ones will decide at once that they need an outing to the toilet.

- Do expect to have fun yourself and be open to learn. The teaching aspect of the programme is not just for the kids—God may choose to speak to you too!
- Do use your common sense!
- Don't loiter on the edge, chatting or distracting the children or presenter, as the programme is taking place.

Safety guidelines

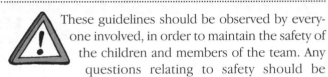 These guidelines should be observed by everyone involved, in order to maintain the safety of the children and members of the team. Any questions relating to safety should be addressed to the organizers before problems arise.

- No team member should be alone with a child where their activity cannot be seen by others.
- Always treat the children with respect and dignity.
- Never use physical punishment.
- Ensure that more than one person is present if a child needs to be washed or helped in the toilet.
- Don't become over-friendly, with children sitting on your lap, hugging or rough-and-tumbling.
- Team members should avoid any inappropriate touching or any excessively rough or physical games. Don't play-fight children, or join in games where you could fall on a child, or run around with children on your shoulders.
- Do not engage in any scapegoating, ridicule or rejection of a child.
- Do not invite a child to your home alone.
- Avoid giving lifts to children on their own, other than for short journeys or in an emergency. If you do need to do so, the child should sit on a rear seat of the car, using an appropriate seat belt.

- If you contact a child in your group during or after the holiday club, ensure that you identify yourself as a member of the holiday club team
- If abuse is suspected, do not encourage the child to talk further. Report suspicions immediately to the holiday club co-ordinator and make written notes of anything you and the child said to each other.

Fire safety

- Do not use candles, matches or lighters on the premises.
- Familiarize yourself with the fire exits.
- Observe fire drills—they are for everybody's safety.

Stay legal

- If your holiday club lasts for more than two hours and runs for six days or more in a year, then you need to register with Social Services. If you are planning follow-up events, this rule might affect you.
- If under-8s are involved, write to inform Social Services of your plans.
- Have someone on security to stop children or strangers from wandering in or out.

For further information about legal requirements for child protection, contact your local council, your diocese or church office, or:

The Churches' Child Protection Advisory Service
Disclosure Service
PO Box 133
Swanley
Kent
BR8 7UQ

Tel: 0845 120 4549
Fax: 0845 120 4552
E-mail: disclosure@ccpas.co.uk
Website: www.ccpas.co.uk

Daily programmes

The apostle Paul says that the Christian life is like an athlete running a race, and that Jesus is the Ultimate Champion. This holiday club programme looks at the life of Jesus and how he 'ran the race'. It encourages children also to run the race, in order to receive the prize that God has waiting for us.

A true athlete has…

- *direction*: being focused and having his or her eyes fixed on the finish line
- to avoid *distraction*: it's easy to be tempted off course, but we must remain on track
- total *dedication* to the sport, to the coach and to the rest of the team
- great *determination*: there will be many hurdles and painful experiences to overcome along the way
- *decoration* to look forward to as they climb the podium to receive their glorious prize: the prize is available for everyone who stays on course!

Day One: Direction

The younger we start the race, the better. Jesus didn't just suddenly appear as a grown-up man, but started life as we all do—as a tiny baby.

Memory verse: 'Let us run with determination the race that lies before us. Let us keep our eyes fixed on Jesus in whom our faith depends.' (Hebrews 12:1–2)
Bible story: The boy Jesus in the temple (Luke 2:41 –52)

Day Two: Distraction

Before Jesus began his work for God, he was tempted to turn away from the true course. If he had cheated and opted for the easy route, he would not have been a true champion. But he remained on course and won the race!

Memory verse: 'Keep yourself in training for a godly life!' (1 Timothy 4:7)
Bible story: The temptation of Jesus (Matthew 4:1–12)

Day Three: Dedication

Jesus was dedicated to God and to other people. He prayed regularly to God, asking for guidance, in the same way that an athlete listens to the coach and puts his advice into practice.

Memory verse: 'Encourage one another and help one another!' (1 Thessalonians 5:11)
Bible story: Jesus heals a paralysed man (Mark 2:1–12)

Day Four: Determination

Jesus overcame many hurdles. He remained faithful to the race despite having to face the cross.

Memory verse: 'If God is for us, who can be against us?' (Romans 8:31)
Bible story: Jesus' death and resurrection (Mark 15 and 16; John 20:1–23)

Day Five: Decoration

Jesus ascended to heaven in victory. He had stayed the course and was exalted to the highest place.

Memory verse: I'm gonna run straight towards the goal in order to win the prize, the prize that the Lord will give me on that day!' (Based on Philippians 3:14 and 2 Timothy 4:8)
Bible story: Jesus is taken up to heaven and is exalted to the highest place—alive and victorious! (Luke 24:50–53; Acts 1:1–11)

Timetable

A two-and-a-half-hour programme (adaptable to suit your situation)

9.15am Team meets together to pray.

9.35am Last-minute preparation.

9.45am Open doors for registration. Split the children into three teams according to their ages. Children go to team leaders / areas.

10.00am Stage-based presentation/Up-front time 1 (30 minutes).
- Introduction and welcome
- Theme song (songs available on *High-energy holiday club songs* CD See final page for details)
- Action song
- Theme illustration
- Memory verse song
- Watt family daily drama
- Song or memory verse recap

10.30am Activity time. Three activities, each lasting for 25 minutes. In their teams the children rotate round the different activities so that all the children do each activity.
- Game
- Craft
- Snack, chat and funsheet

12.00pm Stage-based presentation/Up-front time 2 (30 minutes).
- Songs
- Puppet sketch
- Memory verse recap
- Quick quiz
- Bible story
- Round-up/prayer
- Theme song

12.30pm Children go back to small groups and wait to be collected.

Reproduced with permission from *Champions!* published by BRF 2004 (1 84101 185 1)

Champions! theme song

John Hardwick

The Watt Family theme song

John Hardwick

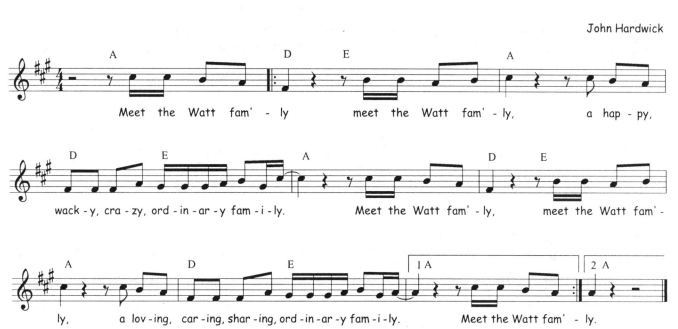

Meet the Watt fam' - ly   meet the Watt fam' - ly,   a hap - py,

wack - y, cra - zy, ord - in - ar - y fam - i - ly.   Meet the Watt fam' - ly,   meet the Watt fam' -

ly,   a lov - ing, car - ing, shar - ing, ord - in - ar - y fam - i - ly.   Meet the Watt fam' - ly.

Champions! memory verse songs

These songs are based on the text of the Good News Bible. However, they do not necessarily include the whole verse, and wording may vary slightly to fit the melody.

--- *Day One* ---

Direction

Let us run with determination

John Hardwick

Distraction

Keep yourself in training

John Hardwick

In the first book of Ti - mo - thy   In the first book of Ti - mo - thy

Chap - ter four verse se - ven;   Chap - ter four verse se - ven; says, 'Keep your - self in train - ing' says,

'Keep your - self in train - ing'   'for a god - ly life'.   'for a god - ly life'.

Dedication

Encourage one another

John Hardwick

One Thes -sa - lo - ni -ans, One___ Thes -sa - lo - ni -ans, One Thes -sa - lo - ni - ans five___

___verse e - le - ven. One Thes -sa - lo - ni -ans, One___ Thes -sa - lo - ni -ans chap -ter five___ verse

e - le - ven. ___ e - le - ven. ___ En - cou -rage one,___ en - cou - rage one an -o - ther.

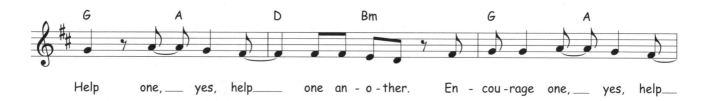

Help   one,___ yes, help___ one an - o -ther. En - cou -rage one, ___ yes, help___

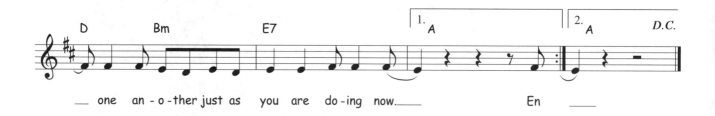

___ one an - o -ther just as you are do -ing now.___ En ___

Determination

God is for us

John Hardwick

Decoration

Running in the race

John Hardwick

Theme illustrations

Day One: Direction

Choose two volunteers who are about the same weight and similar strength. (For the purpose of explaining the illustration, we'll call them Jack and Jill.) Try to choose the volunteers from the 8-to-10 age group.

Jack and Jill stand facing each other, with a rubber ring between them (a dog's toy 'tug of war' rubber ring would be fine). They each hold on to the rubber ring with one hand, leaving their other hand free to reach out behind them.

Ask a leader to stand about two metres behind Jack, holding a bowl containing three sweets for him. Ask a second leader to stand about two metres behind Jill, holding a bowl containing three sweets for her.

Tell Jack and Jill that they have 30 seconds to get as many sweets as possible out of their own bowl. They are only allowed to collect one sweet at a time, so each time they get one, they have to return to the centre point.

Jack and Jill will automatically think that this means a 'tug of war' and will pull against each other. The 30 seconds will probably pass very quickly, with Jack and Jill struggling to get even one of their sweets, let alone all three!

When they have failed, tell them that it is possible for them both to manage to get all three of their sweets. How is this possible? The clue is that if Jack and Jill move together in the same direction, taking turns to travel together to each other's bowl, the goal can be achieved. Let them try again, this time working together and travelling in the same direction.

God gives us all the gift of life. He wants to walk with us but often we ignore him and go off in the opposite direction. Let's choose to travel life's journey with God, moving in the same direction as him.

Day Two: Distraction

Ask for a volunteer. Show them a wrapped present, and tell them that this is their prize if they really want it. Say that you're not sure what it is, but you're sure it's something special because (name of holiday club organizer) has brought it as a special holiday club prize. Give it to them, but don't let them open it at this stage.

Then say to the volunteer that, actually, you'd quite like the present, and offer to swap a sweet for it. Hopefully, they will say 'No', so then offer them a small chocolate bar. If they still say 'No', then offer them a bigger chocolate bar.

Hopefully, they will still refuse to swap with you and you will have failed to distract them from the main prize. Now invite them to open the wrapped present. A great holiday club prize could be the *High-energy holiday club songs* CD (see final page for details). Thank goodness the volunteer didn't swap—they would have missed out on a great prize!

God wants us to travel life's journey with him. He wants us to do what is right and not what is wrong. He also wants us to love, obey and follow him. If we do this, then he promises us a special prize. But some people may try to tempt us off course and try to persuade us to do things that are wrong. They may try to distract us away from following God. But we mustn't let them! We must keep going and keep following and one day we will receive God's prize.

Day Three: Dedication

Try to get hold of some musical instruments—for example, a violin, flute, guitar, piano or whatever is available. Do not mention the musical instruments at this stage. Ask for as many volunteers as you have musical instruments. Give each volunteer one of the instruments

and, in turn, ask them to play it. Of course, you hope that they won't be able to do so. Explain that to play a musical instrument takes a lot of practice and dedication!

Then ask all the volunteers to play the instruments together. The result will not be beautiful music, but a noisy cacophony. If there are people available who can play the instruments, ask them to come and demonstrate, listening to one at a time. Then ask them all to play something together. If there are no musicians available, then play a CD of a piece of music that includes those instruments. Musical instruments can be harmonic or disharmonic!

To become a musician takes a lot of practice and dedication. To be a band takes teamwork—all having a part to play and valuing one another's input. To become a champion for Jesus will take dedication. We can't afford to give up. But God has provided the Church to help us—a place where people should value one another and where we all have a part to play.

church — encouragement
help

Day Four: Determination

Ask for two volunteers who are friends of each other. Ask one of the volunteers how special the other one is to them. Would that one be prepared to give a piggyback to their friend and carry them the length of the hall or stage? Hopefully, they will say 'Yes'. Ask them if they would still be prepared to do this if someone was to squirt them with a water pistol as they did so. If they still say 'Yes', then let them try.

NB: Safety first! If the friends are not of equal height and weight, don't allow the smaller of the two to carry the larger.

The first person was prepared to carry his/her friend and allow himself/herself to be squirted as s/he did so. The person went through that struggle for a friend! Jesus loves us so much that he was prepared to die for us on the cross. He went through all that for us. Thank you, Jesus!

Day Five: Decoration

Set up a little obstacle course. Choose one volunteer from each of the age groups, and say that you are going to time each one of them to see how long it takes them to complete the course.

After they have all been timed, give the results. Even though all the times were different and the oldest child probably completed the course in the shortest time, say, 'In first place was (volunteer's name).' Give that person a gold medal. Then say, 'In first [not second!] place was (next volunteer's name).' Give that person a gold medal, Then repeat again, 'In first place was (third volunteer's name)', and give that person a gold medal.

When it comes to running life's race, God is not interested in how rich we have become or whether or not we are famous. He's interested in how we lived our lives. Have we been kind and have we gone out of our way to help others? But also, have we chosen to follow him and thanked him for all he has done for us? If we have, then we are champions. There are no first, second and third places; we are all winners and he has a prize waiting for us.

The Watt Family daily dramas

The Watt family adventure serial drama has proved to be a real winner in John Hardwick's holiday club programmes. Children love the different characters and can't wait for the next adventure the following day, proving the formula to be a real incentive for the children to return. Although the drama does have links with the *Champions!* theme, the main aim of the drama is that it should be fun, rather than being taken too seriously.

In this story, Grandma, Rick and Wendy have won a competition. They receive a free holiday to go and see the Olympic games. While they are there, they are introduced to the British team coach, who seems a little preoccupied. Some of the top British athletes have gone missing. The Watt family help to sort out the situation and end up becoming true champions!

Day One: Direction

Cast
Narrator (a competent reader,
who keeps the story going)
Grandma Watt (a wacky, fun-loving character)
Rick Watt (loves adventure)
Wendy Watt (could talk for England!)

Props
Teapot and mugs
Water pistol
A letter
Telephone

Scene: A room in the Watt family's home. The stage could be set out with the family sitting around a dining-table with a teapot and mugs for Grandma and the rest of the

family. Play and sing the Watt family theme song. This gives you time to set up the stage and for the actors to take up positions on stage. The children will also enjoy singing along each day to this simple song.

Narrator: Meet the Watt family! A happy, wacky, crazy, ordinary family. Meet the Watt family, a loving, caring, sharing, ordinary family. Oh, where are they?

Wendy: *(Wendy bounces in, full of life.)* Hi! They say I talk a lot, but I don't really… I don't talk any more than anyone else. Unless no one else is talking—then I may as well make the most of the chance!

Narrator: Be quiet, Wendy! Here comes Rick.

Rick: *(Comes in like James Bond, with water pistol in hand, humming the James Bond theme music. Squirts Wendy and narrator, then the audience)* Hi, I'm Watt. Rick Watt! And this is my super-soaker which I use to squirt squirts with! Well, actually, it's not a super-soaker— Grandma borrowed that to squirt the dogs that chased the cats. Then to squirt the cats that chase the birds. Then to squirt the birds that catch the worms. I'm sure I saw her trying to squirt the worms the other day! But now she's lost my super-soaker, so I just have an ordinary water pistol instead.

Narrator: Where's your grandma?

Wendy: She went out on her motorbike, but she was sitting on it the wrong way round, complaining that someone had stolen her handlebars again. She's always getting lost— she hasn't got a very good sense of direction at all.

Rick: No wonder. Have you seen her atlas? It was printed in 1905! She says that she doesn't trust the new ones, because there are too many blue and red lines.

Narrator:	Here she comes now. Did you enjoy your ride, Grandma?
Grandma:	Someone's stolen the handlebars again!
Wendy:	Grandma, why can't you just knit like everyone else's grandmas?
Grandma:	It's too hard. I left it too late to learn how to do that. You need to learn to do things like that when you're younger.
Narrator:	Is that the postman I hear?
Grandma:	Pardon?
Wendy and Rick:	Post!

Both Wendy and Rick dash to get to the post first. Wendy gets to it, then Rick chases Wendy round Grandma, grabs the letter, then runs back the other way, holding the letter above his head. Grandma takes letter but neither Rick nor Wendy notice and carry on running round. Grandma walks away and starts to open the letter.

Grandma:	Here, Wendy, can you read this? I can't find my glasses anywhere.
Narrator:	You're wearing them!
Rick and Wendy:	*(Both look amazed)* How did you get that letter?
Wendy:	*(Reading the letter)* Seems we've won a holiday. To the Olympic games.
Rick:	Along with another million families!
Wendy:	No, this is genuine! Phone this number to find out more details!
Rick:	*(Phones number)* 0... 0... 7. Hello, this is Watt, Rick Watt. Have we won the holiday to the Olympic games? ... Yes! Wow! When do we go? ... Tomorrow's fine, yes. *(Replaces phone)* Hey, we'd better start packing.
Narrator:	So Wendy, Rick and Grandma start to pack for the holiday of a lifetime. Will Wendy ever stop

talking? Will Grandma ever know where she is going and manage to sit on her motorbike facing in the right direction? Will Rick be allowed through Customs with his water pistol? Will Wendy and Rick be allowed through Customs with Grandma? Find out what happens tomorrow!

Play the Watt family theme music.

Day Two: Distraction

Cast
Narrator
Grandma Watt
Rick Watt
Wendy Watt
The British team coach (wears a blazer or jacket and badge saying 'British Coach')

Props
Bunting
A selection of national flags
Water pistol
Mobile phone
Walking-stick

Scene: The stage is set with some bunting, or some national flags. These could be painted on to sheets of paper and strung across the stage. You may also like to paint some flats to resemble a stadium backdrop, showing the Olympic rings and seated areas with the crowds watching the events.

Narrator:	You may remember that Rick, Wendy and Grandma have won a holiday to the Olympic games. Despite an eventful journey, they have made it safe and sound.
Rick:	Wow! What an exciting journey.
Grandma:	Yes, Rick, you really shouldn't have gone to the plane's cockpit to ask the pilot if he could fly it with his eyes closed!
Wendy:	Yes, you're not meant to distract the pilot like that. The plane went all over the place. It became a very moving journey for many.
Rick:	She means they were feeling sick!
Grandma:	What did you have to bring that up for?
Rick:	Anyway, Grandma, at least I didn't start copying the air hostess when she was going through the safety routine.
Wendy:	Yes, it was very distracting for the rest of the passengers. They were all laughing at you rather than watching the air hostess! It was most embarrassing.

Grandma: I thought she was leading a keep-fit class. I wondered why no one else was joining in! Anyway, we're here now, so where do we have to go now, Wendy?

Wendy: Well, because we are the special prize winners, we've been invited to meet the British team coach.

Rick: Oh, brilliant! We're going to meet the actual British team coach!

Grandma: What's so exciting about that? I haven't come all this way just to go to some coach station to meet a bus! I don't care how posh it is!

Wendy: There he is now!

Grandma: Don't be silly, he's not a bus! What does he do—give all the team piggy-backs?

Wendy: Be quiet, Grandma, he might hear you.

They all run across to the coach, who is wearing a badge saying 'British Coach'

Grandma: He still doesn't look like a coach to me.

Wendy: Hi, we're the Watt family!

Coach: *(Looking confused)* What family?

Grandma: That's right, the Watt Family. I'm Grandma Watt.

Coach: What?

All: Don't say 'what', say 'pardon'!

Rick: I'm Rick Watt.

Coach: Who?

Wendy: No, not Who, Watt! We have got some relatives called 'Who' but we're the Watts. I'm Wendy Watt.

Coach: Oh, you're the prize winners—the Watt family. Why didn't you say so?

All: We did!

Coach's mobile phone rings.

Coach: Excuse me a second. *(Speaks into phone)* Hi. What?

All: Yes?

Coach: *(To Watt family)* No, not you! *(Back to phone)* Say that again. The pole vaulter and the shot putter are still missing? Well, there's only one thing we can do!

Grandma: Panic!

Coach: *(To Grandma)* Be quiet! *(Into phone)* No, not you! Well, we'll just have to sit tight. Keep me informed. Must go! *(To Watt family)* Oh dear, our two top athletes have gone missing.

Rick: Don't worry, Coach, if they don't turn up, Grandma can do the pole-vaulting.

Grandma: What's revolting?

Rick: And I'll do the shot-putting! *(Squirts coach with water pistol)*

Coach: *(Sarcastically)* Very funny. I can hardly see your grandma being able to jump over a four-metre bar.

Wendy: Don't under-estimate her. Her washing-line is about that high. Hey, Grandma, show him your party trick with your walking-stick.

Grandma: OK!

Rick lies on the floor and Grandma runs along with the stick in the air, then uses her walking-stick to boost herself over Rick.

Coach: Err, yes! What can I say to that? These are top athletes who have been in training ever since they were children. *(Phone rings)* Hello… Who is this? … You've kidnapped our athletes!

All: *(Freeze, look shocked and chant)* Dum! Dum! Dum!

Narrator: Oh dear! What will the coach do? Will the athletes be rescued or will Grandma have to do the pole-vaulting after all? Is Grandma still confused about Coach looking nothing like a bus? Is there a 'fastest talker' competition? At least we would win one gold medal, with Wendy on our side! Find out what happens tomorrow!

Play the Watt family theme music.

Day Three: Dedication

Cast
Narrator
Grandma Watt
Rick Watt
Wendy Watt
The British team coach
Mr Steel (a baddie)

Reproduced with permission from *Champions!* published by BRF 2004 (1 84101 185 1)

....
Props
Bunting
A selection of national flags
Water pistol
Mobile phone
Walking-stick
Bandit's mask
Two signs *(see script for details)*
....

Scene: As on Day Two, the stage is set with some bunting, or some national flags. These could be painted on to sheets of paper and strung across the stage. You may also like to paint some flats to resemble a stadium backdrop, showing the seated areas with the crowds watching the track.

Narrator: The two top British athletes have been kidnapped by a man calling himself Mr Steel. The British team coach is in a panic!

Coach: I know, I'll phone the Prime Minister and see what he suggests! *(Dials and then speaks on the phone)* Hello, Sir, British team coach here. I'm afraid we've got a problem. Seems we've lost our top athletes. Any suggestions? … No, it wasn't very careless of me! … What do you mean, 'Can't you get some more?' You don't understand—they've been kidnapped! … He's gone! *(Phone rings again)* Hello again, Sir. … Sorry? … You're not the PM, you're Mr Steel? Ooh-er!

All: *(Look shocked and chant)* Dum! Dum! Dum!

Grandma: Give it to me. I'll sort him out. *(Takes phone)* Now look here, you're being a very naughty little boy!

Rick: Give it to me. I'll sort him. *(Goes to squirt phone with water pistol)*

Wendy: Don't be silly. Give it to me. I'll sort him out. Now look here, Mr Steel. You may think you're clever, but you're not! You haven't got

our top athletes at all—no, no, no—just the reserve ones. We have the best athlete in the world—brilliant at everything, top in all sports. This person is so precious that we have disguised her… Pardon? … What as? Well, I'm not going to tell you that, am I? I'm not that stupid. But you'll never find her in her grey wig, skirt and walking-stick, and I certainly won't tell you that her code name is Grandma Watt. So you can keep the reserve athletes! *(Hangs up)*

Rick: That's telling them!

Grandma: Sounds like me. What have you done? They'll be after me now too!

Rick: Good idea. No one to tell us what to do!

Grandma: Thanks a lot. I thought you loved me.

Wendy: We do!

Rick: Yes! When they come for you, we'll jump on them, squirt them and force them to tell us where the real athletes are.

Coach: My word, what dedication! You're prepared to risk your Grandma for the sake of the nation! What pride!

Grandma: Oh dear, oh dear! All this excitement means I need the loo!

Coach: The ladies' is just across the courtyard.

Rick, Wendy and the team coach wander off stage and Grandma mimes wandering through door and across the courtyard. Mr Steel comes on stage wearing a bandit's mask. He lifts a sign saying 'I'm a baddie, so boo!' Grandma lifts a sign saying 'I'm a goodie, so cheer!' Each of them takes it in turns to lift and lower their signs, with audience booing and cheering as appropriate.

Mr Steel: Are you Grandma Watt?

Grandma: How did you know? Do you know me? *(Looking at Mr Steel hard)* You need to get more sleep. You've got dark circles round your eyes.

Mr Steel: That's my mask!

Grandma: Your mask? Well, fancy leaving your face mask on! Have you just got out the bath?

Mr Steel: No, I'm a baddie, looking for a granny.

Grandma: Looking for a granny? What is she wearing?

Mr Steel: A wig, a skirt and carrying a walking-stick.

Grandma: Well, I can't see one!

Mr Steel: Hey! It's you!

Chase begins. Then Grandma and Mr Steel stop and freeze.

Narrator: What will happen to Grandma? Will she be caught or will Rick and Wendy rescue her? Is it really right to boo like that? Find out what will happen in tomorrow's exciting episode of the Watt family.

Play the Watt family theme music.

Day Four: Determination

Cast
Narrator
Grandma Watt
Rick Watt
Wendy Watt
The British team coach
Mr Steel (a baddie)
Two athletes

Props
Bunting
A selection of national flags
Water pistol
Mobile phone
Walking-stick
Bandit's mask
A wig, glasses and skirt

Scene: As on Day Two, the stage is set with some bunting, or some national flags. These could be painted on to sheets of paper, and strung across the stage. You may also like to paint some flats to resemble a stadium backdrop, showing the seated areas with the crowds watching the track.

Narrator: What has happened to Grandma?

Chase continues—Mr Steel chasing Grandma, then Grandma chasing Mr Steel and so on. Finally, Rick and Wendy come to rescue Grandma. Wendy waves Grandma's walking-stick and Rick shoots his water pistol, but Mr Steel escapes.

Coach: Are you all right?
Grandma: Yes—no thanks to you! Come on, Rick. Come on, Wendy. We're getting out of here. We've come here to have a holiday and that's what we're going to have!
Coach: *(Phone rings)* Oh, it's you again. What? You are willing to exchange the two athletes for that super Grandma athlete you have just fought with? We will need to discuss this. Phone me back in five minutes! *(To Grandma)* Gosh! Well, you certainly fooled him into thinking you're a great athlete. He sounds very determined to make the exchange.
Grandma: He can be as determined as he likes, but I'm off. Let's get out of here—quick!
Rick and Wendy: We can't go now. Our country needs us.
Grandma: Tough! Now, come on!
Coach: Let her go. She's determined to leave.
Rick: But those athletes have a real chance of winning some medals for our country.

Grandma: Oh, so they are more important than me, are they? I should take their place—is that what you're trying to say?
Rick: Yes and no… or no and yes!
Wendy: They are not more important, but you should take their place.
Grandma: No, I shouldn't. Now, come on!
Rick: I'll do it!
Grandma: Don't be silly! I think they may notice the difference between a little boy and a grandma.
Rick: I'll dress up as a grandma. Give me your skirt!
Grandma: Get off! And what will I say to your mum when she phones? 'Oh, they're not here, they've been kidnapped'?
Coach: That's determination for you. He doesn't care if he looks ridiculous or if he may get hurt. He is determined to sacrifice himself for the athletes. Here's a wig, glasses and skirt.
Grandma: What? You will really risk your life for complete strangers? You'll be an ugly grandma!

Wendy: Just like you!
Grandma: Watch it!
Coach: *(Phone rings)* Yes, we're prepared to make the swap.

Mr Steel appears with two athletes. Wendy pushes the real Grandma out of sight. The athletes exchange places with Rick. The athletes are excited to be back.

Athlete 1: Who was the old dear?
Grandma: She's an impostor. They think she's me—a super-granny. Can they be trusted?
Athlete 2: No!
All: Dum! Dum! Dum!
Narrator: Oh no! What have they done? Will we ever see Rick again? And is that so bad? After all, he's a real pain! Find out tomorrow!

Play the Watt family theme music.

Day Five: Decoration

Cast
Narrator
Grandma Watt
Rick Watt
Wendy Watt
The British team coach
Mr Steel
Two athletes

Props
Bunting
A selection of national flags
Water pistol
Mobile phone
Walking-stick
Bandit's mask
A wig, glasses and skirt

Scene: As on Day Two, the stage is set with some bunting, or some national flags. These could be painted on to sheets of paper, and strung across the stage. You may also like to paint some flats to resemble a stadium backdrop, showing the seated areas with the crowds watching the track.

Narrator:	What has happened to Rick? Will they ever see him again? What will the kidnappers do when they realize he's not an athlete, just a silly little boy?
Grandma:	What will happen to Rick when they realize he's just a silly, and very cheeky, little boy?
Wendy:	What will happen to Rick when they realize he's just a silly, very cheeky, and extremely annoying little boy? But we do lo... lo... *(Struggling to say the word 'love')*
Grandma:	What are you trying to say?
Wendy:	We love him.
Grandma:	What's that?
Wendy:	It's a trail of water. Rick must have been shooting a trail of water for us to follow. But is he that bright?
Grandma:	Either that or he's scared stiff and wet himself.
Wendy:	Grandma!
Grandma:	Sorry! Quick, follow that trail before it dries out!

They wander off stage following the trail of water. Mr Steel comes on with Rick dressed as Grandma.

Mr Steel:	So now we have the British secret weapon. Let's see who you are. *(He takes the wig, glasses and skirt off Rick and looks shocked)* Hey, you're just a silly little boy!

Rick:	Ha ha! Yes, we tricked you. I'm just a little boy, so you may as well let me go. *(Puts costume back on)*
Mr Steel:	Never! You will pay for this!
Rick:	*(Pulls out the water pistol)* Hands up!

Mr Steel puts his hands in the air and Rick squirts him. The chase begins. Play traditional chase music. Grandma and Wendy arrive, so Mr Steel finds himself chasing after two grandmas. Wendy trips up Mr Steel. They tie him up and march him off stage. The two athletes and team coach come on stage with gold medals.

Coach:	Well done, guys. You both won the gold. You are champions!

The Watt family come back on to the stage, leading Mr Steel, still tied up.

Coach:	Well done! You've rescued Rick and captured Mr Steel. You guys are the real champions. If it wasn't for your bravery, these athletes wouldn't have been able to compete—and now they have won gold medals. Your country owes you an enormous amount. You're the ones who deserve to be honoured and decorated with a gold medal for bravery!
Grandma:	Stop it! I'll start crying in a minute!
Rick:	No, no, don't stop. I'm enjoying this!
Narrator:	So that's the end of the Watt family adventure. Grandma, Rick and Wendy returned home to a hero's welcome. Rick has become a national heart-throb. Wendy has become a national star—all the girls want to look like her! (Why?) And Grandma is as popular as the Queen! The newspaper headlines read, 'The Watt family—true champions!' What a happy ending!

Play the Watt family theme music.

Champion crafts

Champion folders

You will need
- Thin card or rolls of patterned wallpaper
- Old magazines or catalogues (suitable for collage)
- Scissors
- Rulers
- Glue sticks
- Pencils
- Paints or crayons

Make simple folders for the children to keep activity sheets and other bits and pieces in. Pre-cut the card or wallpaper to measure 34cm x 50cm. You will need one piece per child.

1. Draw a line across the width of the card, 22cm up from the bottom of the length. Draw a second line across the width, 22cm up from the first line (diag. 1).

2. Draw two lines down the length of the paper, 2cm from the edge on each side. Then draw in the diagonals to make flaps as shown. Cut away the shaded area (diag. 2).

3. Fold the paper as shown (diag. 3). Glue the flaps to the back of the folder.

diag. 3

4. Decorate the folder using collage or paints or crayons. The decoration could include Olympic rings, pictures of athletes or flags. Add the child's name and team.

5. Make a sample folder beforehand so that the children can see the finished folder.

diag. 1   **diag. 2**

National flags

You will need
- Sheets of A5 paper
- Garden canes or thin bamboo sticks, 30cm long
- Pencils
- Rulers
- Glue sticks
- Paints or crayons
- Pictures of different flags for reference

Draw a line down one short side of the paper, 2cm from the edge. Fold along line. Mark the design of the flag of your choice on the paper. Mark a corresponding design on the reverse side. Colour the flag. Place the garden cane or bamboo stick inside the folded edge and glue into place.

Countries represented at the Olympic games include Afghanistan, Algeria, Argentina, Australia, Austria, Bolivia, Brazil, Canada, China, Denmark, Ethiopia, Egypt, France, Finland, Germany, Greece, Great Britain, Hungary, Israel, Iceland, India, Italy, Ireland, Japan, Jamaica, Mexico, New Zealand, Nigeria, Russia, Spain, Switzerland, Tanzania, Turkey and the United States.

The Internet is a good source of reference for Olympic flags, and a small amount of time spent on research should provide you with all the information you need for the different designs.

Olympic torch

You will need
- One sheet of A4 paper per child
- Pencils
- Rulers
- Scissors
- Glue sticks or sticky tape
- Yellow paint or crayons
- Red, orange and yellow tissue paper

1. Mark the centre point along one long side of the sheet of paper. Mark a point 5cm down each short side as shown (diag. 1).
2. Draw a curved line from the centre point to the two points on the sides. Cut away the shaded area (diag. 2).
3. Colour the paper. Shape the paper into a cone with the coloured side on the outside, so that the uncut edge

forms the point and the cut edge forms the top as shown (diag. 3). Stick in place.
4. Cut the tissue paper into strips, 24cm x 6cm. Using a selection of colours, push four or five strips of tissue firmly down into the centre of the cone. Glue into place. Scrunch up the strips to form flames as shown (diag. 4).

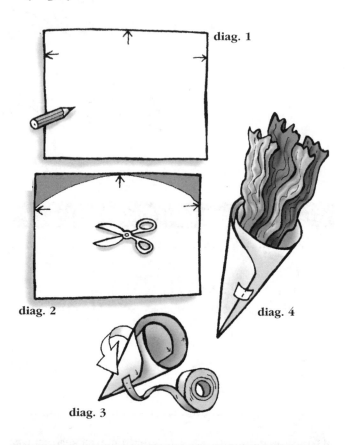

diag. 1

diag. 2

diag. 4

diag. 3

Champion's cup

You will need
- An empty yoghurt pot (washed) per child
- Pipe cleaners (two per child)
- Empty tea packet (one per child)
- Silver foil
- Sticky tape
- Red ribbon

1. Glue the yoghurt pot to the top of the tea packet. Tape one pipe cleaner to each side of the yoghurt pot to form handles.
2. Cover the pipe cleaners, the yoghurt pot and the tea packet with silver foil.
3. Tie the ribbon around the champion's cup as shown.

Edible medals

You will need
- Plain biscuits (Rich Tea or similar)
- Ready-made fondant icing, rolled into small balls
- Yellow food colouring
- Greaseproof paper cut into squares
- Strawberry shoelace sweets

Organize a hand-washing session before this activity. Then give each child a greaseproof paper square, a biscuit, a strawberry shoelace sweet and a ball of fondant icing. Put a few drops of yellow food colouring on to each ball of icing and ask the children to knead it into the icing until the colour is evenly spread throughout the icing.

Place the shoelace sweet at the top of the biscuit to form a loop. Press the icing on to the biscuit to create a smooth surface, covering the biscuit and trapping the ends of the shoelace sweets to secure the loop.

Olympic medals (non-edible!)

You will need
- Circles of thin card, 12cm in diameter (a CD makes a good template)
- Red, white and blue ribbon, cut into 80cm strips
- Sticky tape
- Scissors
- Glue sticks
- Gold, silver and bronze paint

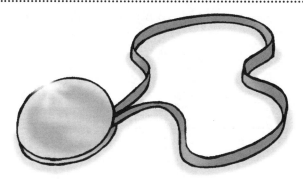

Give each child two card circles. Colour one side of each circle with gold, silver or bronze paint according to choice. Let the paint dry.

When the paint is dry, place the ribbon on the un-coloured side of one circle to form a loop and secure ends with sticky tape.

Place the second circle over the first so that the ribbon ends are in between the two circles and the coloured sides are on the outside. Glue into place.

Decathlon board game

You will need
- Photocopies of the board game on page 65 (one per child)
- Stiff card (A4 sheets)
- Athlete counters cut from template on page 64
- Spinner cut from template on page 64
- Cocktail sticks or spent matchsticks
- Scissors
- Glue sticks
- Paints or crayons
- Felt-tip pens

Give each child a photo-copy of the board game and an A4 sheet of stiff card. Glue the photo-copied sheet to the card. Colour in the game.

Cut out four counters from the template (four per game) and glue to stiff card. Colour the athlete counters according to choice—for example, red, yellow, blue and green.

Cut out the spinner from the template (one per game) and glue to stiff card. Colour the sections of the spinner. Push a cocktail stick or spent matchstick into the centre of the spinner.

The game is now ready to be played. The children will need to be put into groups of four to play the game during the holiday club, or they can take their boards home to try out with their family and friends.

Champions! memory verse mobile

You will need:
- Photocopies of the mobile shapes on pp. 66–68
- Thick cotton thread or twine
- Stiff card
- Colouring pencils or crayons
- Pair of geometry set compasses
- Magazines

Give each child a photocopy of the mobile shape and a sheet of stiff card. Glue the mobile shape to the stiff card and cut out the shape, following the solid lines. Colour in the mobile.

Make a hole in the top of the mobile as shown in the picture below, using the compasses. To avoid injury and protect surfaces, place a magazine underneath the mobile when making the hole. **NB:** Younger children will need adult help.

Cut a length of cotton thread or twine. To complete the mobile, thread a length of cotton or twine through the hole and tie to secure.

Stadium pass

You will need
- Photocopies of the stadium pass template below
- A passport-sized photograph of each child
- Medium-weight card measuring 12cm x 6cm
- Glue sticks
- Felt-tip pens
- Sticky tape (optional)
- Safety pins (optional)

Give each child a piece of card and a copy of the stadium pass template. Glue the template to the card.

Draw the flag of your country in the space at the top-left of the pass, and colour it in.

Glue the photograph of the child in the space provided at the right-hand-side of the pass. Write the child's name and team on the lines.

The stadium pass can be transformed into a badge by securing a safety pin to the reverse side using sticky tape.

Olympic twirler

You will need
- Circles of medium-weight card, 12cm in diameter (a CD makes a good template)
- Pair of geometry set compasses
- Magazines
- Pencils
- Rulers
- Lengths of wool or string (not nylon, as this can cut into the hand)
- Paints, crayons or coloured pencils (blue, yellow, black, green and red)

It is said that the five Olympic rings represent the five major regions of the world—Africa, the Americas, Asia, Europe and Oceania. Every national flag in the world includes at least one of the five colours, which are (from left to right) blue, yellow, black, green and red.

1. Give each child a card circle and divide it into seven equal sections. Colour five of the sections with a different colour of the Olympic rings—blue, yellow, black, green and red. Leave two sections white.
2. Make two holes either side of the centre as shown (see p. 31), using the compasses. To avoid injury and to protect surfaces, place a magazine underneath the card when making the hole. **NB:** Younger children will need adult help.

Name: _____

Team: _____

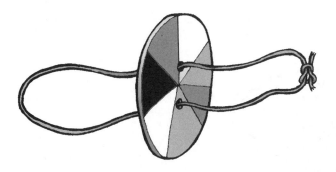

Cut carefully along the dotted lines

3. Cut a length of wool or string about 60cm long and thread it through the holes in the card. Tie the ends together to make a long loop.

4. Holding an end of the loop in each hand, fairly taut, twirl hands in a circle until the wool or string is well twisted. Then, moving both hands together and apart, the disc will start to spin.

5. Watch the colours of the Olympic ring become one as the disc spins. This is a good illustration of all nations uniting through sport.

Insert the javelin and fix with a split-pin fastener

Moving athlete card

You will need
- Photocopies of the javelin-thrower (page 69) and the javelin (this page), on paper or thin card
- Scissors
- Coloured pencils, crayons or felt-tip pens
- Split-pin fasteners

Colour in the picture of the athlete and javelin.

Assemble the card as shown opposite.

NB: Younger children will need adult help.

X

31

Champion games

True champions

Divide the children into teams with a maximum of 13 children in each team. Each team lines up, ready for a relay race. Each child runs down the course and collects one letter from a tray. The letters are then sorted to form the words 'TRUE CHAMPIONS'. (There are 13 letters in total.) The first team to collect all the letters, spell out the right phrase and be sitting in a straight line is the winner.

If you have fewer than 13 children in the team, allow some to run more than once until all the letters are collected.

To add further interest to the game, arrange an obstacle course between the starting line and the tray of letters. The course could be like this: run down to a cone and run right round it, run to a hoop and go through it, run to another cone and run right round this one, then run and collect one letter from a tray. The children then run straight back to their team and the second child sets off in the same way.

'Come on, team!'

Split the children into two equal teams. One team forms a circle facing inwards. A leader stands in the middle of the circle with a ball. The other team lines up behind a cone. When you say 'Go!' the leader starts to throw the ball to each child in the circle in turn, with each child throwing it back. The leader counts how many throws are made.

At the same time, the first child from the other team runs to and around the circle of children and back. The second child then does the same. Once the second team have all run, shout 'Stop!' When this happens, note the number of throws that were made by the first team.

The teams swap places and repeat the game. The winning team is the one that made the most throws and therefore worked better together as a team.

'Sorry, sold out!' The shopping race

Explain to the children that they are the athletes at the Olympics, but they've forgotten some of their equipment and need to go shopping to try to buy the missing items.

Make a master list of 20 pieces of equipment. The list could include:

- Javelin
- Running shoes
- Discus
- Boxing gloves
- Hockey stick
- Tennis racket
- Fencing foil (sword)
- Football
- Dumbbells
- Swimming goggles
- Golf clubs
- Starting pistol
- Shorts
- Swimming costume
- Football boots
- Safety helmet
- Stopwatch
- Whistle
- Tracksuit
- First aid kit

Divide the master list into four shops as follows:

1. Javelin, hockey stick, dumbbells, shorts, stopwatch
2. Running shoes, tennis racket, swimming goggles, swimming costume, whistle
3. Discus, fencing foil, golf clubs, safety helmet, tracksuit
4. Boxing gloves, football, starting pistol, football boots, first aid kit

Give one list to each of four leaders (the shopkeepers). Each leader stands in a corner of the room on a chair. Do not tell the children which leader is 'selling' which item.

The children stand in the middle. Call out one object from the master list. The children then have to go to each shopkeeper and ask, 'Do you sell…?' If the shopkeeper says 'No', then the child has to ask another shopkeeper. Once the children have found the shop selling the item, they form a queue. The last five children to join the queue are out of the game. 'Sorry, sold out!'

Peg it!

Split the children into teams of five. Give each team a tray, a dice and five pegs.

Play some music. While the music is playing, the children in each team take it in turn to throw the dice. If they throw a six, they are allowed to take one peg off any other team. The teams are not allowed to defend the pegs. After three or four minutes, stop the music. The team with the most pegs is the winner of that round.

You've probably got time to play again, so restore the pegs to five per team, play the music and *Peg it!*

The Watt family story game

Split the children into teams of ten. Sit them in a straight line facing the front. Give each child a character name as follows:

Child 1: Grandma
Child 2: Rick
Child 3: Wendy
Child 4: Coach
Child 5: Shot putter
Child 6: Pole vaulter
Child 7: Long jumper
Child 8: Swimmer
Child 9: Javelin thrower
Child 10: Mr Steel

Read the story below, slowly. Every time the children hear their character name, they stand up, step out of the line to their left, run round the front of the line, then down the back of the line and back round to their place. Carry on reading the story slowly so that there are always children running.

Grandma Watt received a letter. It was an invitation to go to the Olympic games! **Rick Watt** and **Wendy Watt** were invited too!

When they arrived, the **coach** of the British team came to meet them. He looked worried. 'My champion **shot putter** has got something in his eye and can't put the shot any more. My **pole vaulter** has decided she is now scared of heights, and the **long jumper** jumped so far, he's completely disappeared!

My champion **swimmer** is convinced she saw a shark in the pool and won't get in. My **javelin**

33

thrower threw the javelin too high—it landed in a hot-air balloon and hasn't been seen since. And now I hear that **Mr Steel** intends to steal my top athletes. 'What shall I do?' wailed the **coach**.

'Don't ask me,' said **Grandma**. 'I need a cup of tea before I can do anything.'

Wendy was far more positive. 'If the **shot putter** can't put the shot, then maybe the **pole vaulter** can instead! And I'm sure I just saw the **long jumper** jump the swimming pool! Maybe **Rick** can get another javelin for the **javelin thrower** and they can hunt for the shark in the pool. Champion **swimmer**, would you mind making a cup of tea for **Grandma**? It looks like she's knitting a **long jumper** for the **coach**!'

Suddenly, **Mr Steel** appeared, carrying the teapot and teabags. 'Ha,' he said, 'no more tea for any of you again!'

'Get him!' shouted the **coach**.

The **shot putter** forgot all about his bad eye and took up the chase. The **swimmer** dived into the pool and swam her fastest length ever, shouting, 'No one steals **Grandma's** teabags and gets away with it!'

But still **Mr Steel** kept running. **Rick** sprinted down the track like a speeding bull, and the **coach** was very impressed. **Wendy** stopped bossing everybody else about and also joined in the chase. The **pole vaulter** looked up from trying to put the shot. The **javelin thrower** threw his spare javelin, pinning **Mr Steel's** shirt to the post, but he wriggled free and carried on running. Finally, to everyone surprise, the **pole vaulter** took the pole and jumped high into the air, landing on the back of **Mr Steel**! **Grandma** grabbed her teabags from him and made a nice cup of tea.

Then, **Rick**, **Wendy**, the **coach**, the **shot putter**, the **long jumper**, the **swimmer**, the **javelin thrower**, **Grandma** and even **Mr Steel** all cheered the **pole vaulter**, who had just made the highest jump ever!

The end.

Puppet sketches

Day One: Direction

Bert: Tell me it's not true.

Lucy: It's not true!

Bert: Thank goodness for that! How embarrassing for you if it had been true!

Lucy: What? I don't know what you're talking about.

Bert: You don't? I thought you did. Shaz said that you were disqualified from the cross-country race because you ran in the wrong direction round the course. But I said that not even you could be that silly!

Lucy:: It wasn't my fault. I wasn't there at the start, so I missed the instructions. I was late, so Dad just dropped me off and I started running round the course the same way as it was last year.

Bert: What? So it's true, then!

Lucy: Yes, but don't tell anyone, especially this lot *(meaning audience)*. It's so embarrassing!

Bert: Err, too late!

Lucy: Oh yes. Anyway, I went round this one tree and smack, bang, wallop! I ran straight into the race leader!

Bert: Ouch!

Lucy: It certainly was! I shouted at her for going in the wrong direction and then carried on my way, round the next bend, and then smack, bang, wallop!

Bert: Ouch!

Lucy: Yep! I ran into the next runner! I shouted at her, then carried on my way. You'll never guess what happened next.

Bert: You ran into the next runner!

Lucy: Wow! How did you know? That's when I realized that they must have changed the direction of the race this year.

Bert: If you'd been there at the start, you would have known. Great athletes are focused and know which way they are meant to be going!

Lucy: All right! Don't rub it in! I'm off for a soak in the bath. My poor legs have massive bruises after running into all the other runners. Bye, everyone.

Bert: Wait for me! Bye, everyone!

Day Two: Distraction

Lucy: *(To Bert)* We need to buy my mum some chocolates.

Bert: Yeah, and a card!

Lucy: *(To audience)* It was my mum's birthday yesterday. She's ever so old. She's 30!

Bert: No she's not, she's 21. She told me, and your mum wouldn't lie!

Lucy: Oh! Anyway, I decided, seeing it was her birthday, to take her breakfast in bed. I made toast.

Bert: Is that what the burning smell was when I came in?

Lucy: Er… yeah! I put the toast under the grill, but then I was distracted.

Bert: How come?

Lucy: When you've got to go, then you've got to go!

Bert: Where?

Lucy: Do I have to spell it out? To the toilet! When I got back, the toast was, er… what's the word?

Bert: Cremated!

Lucy: Mum said that it was the thought that counted! I told her to have a lie-in, seeing it was her birthday. That's when you came round, Bert.

Bert: *(To audience)* Yeah, we'd planned it before-hand. While she was in bed, we would make her a birthday cake.

Reproduced with permission from *Champions!* published by BRF 2004 (1 84101 185 1)

Lucy:	We got out the bowls, ten of them in all. There was one for the margarine.
Bert:	Another for the eggs.
Lucy:	Yes, Bert! He decided to show off and threw an egg in the air.
Bert:	I would have caught it if you hadn't made me jump.
Lucy:	It was hardly my fault that you dropped it. I wasn't messing around. I was carefully spooning out the flour.
Bert:	Yeah! But a wasp landed on her hand and she panicked, flicked her hand, and the flour went all over me, and the floor!
Lucy:	Anyway, we finally finished mixing the cake and put it in the oven. It was going to take 45 minutes to bake.
Bert:	That was when we should have tidied up and done the washing-up.
Lucy:	Yes. But disaster struck! Why did you have to distract me?
Bert:	Me, distract you? You distracted me!
Lucy:	I only asked you if you wanted a go on my roller skates.
Bert:	And I only said, 'Wow! Yes, please.'
Lucy:	We had lots of fun for an hour or so…
Bert:	Yep! You've guessed it!
Lucy:	We forget all about the mess and the washing-up.

Bert:	And the birthday cake and your mum!
Lucy:	Oh boy, were we in trouble! Why do you always distract me? Now we've got to go and clean up the mess—and make a new cake, as the first one came out rather dark.
Bert:	Yeah, cremated! But before we do, I've been dying to show you my new computer game…

Lucy:	Arrgh… you're doing it again!
Bert:	What?
Lucy:	Distracting me! We'd be great kids if we didn't get distracted so easily.
Bert:	You sound just like your mum!
Both:	Bye!

Day Three: Dedication

Lucy:	Hey, Bert! You know that cross-country race I was in?
Bert:	The one where you went the wrong way round the course?
Lucy:	All right, don't go on about it! You'll never guess who actually won.
Bert:	Watt?
Lucy:	What?
Bert:	Not what… Watt. Was it Watt… Wendy Watt?
Lucy:	No, no. She's a good runner, but we all thought it was going to be Lizzie Long. She's won it for two years on the trot and was telling everyone that she was fitter and faster than ever.
Bert:	So did she win?
Lucy:	Well, that's just the thing. It was turning out to be a really close race between Lizzie and Tina Turbo.
Bert:	Well, it's always close between those two.
Lucy:	Yes, Tina Turbo was in the lead, with Lizzie Long right on her heels. Suddenly Tina tripped over a log and Lizzie then tripped over her.
Bert:	Ouch! I bet Lizzie was mad.
Lucy:	She was at first, but she got up and carried on running. Then she realized that Tina hadn't got up.
Bert:	Gosh! So Lizzie had a clear run. She must have won easily.
Lucy:	No! Slow slug Susie won.
Bert:	What? How come?
Lucy:	Well, Lizzie Long looked back and realized that Tina Turbo was still face down in the mud!
Bert:	Don't trust her! It would have been just a trick. I bet as soon as Lizzie Long went over, Tina Turbo got up and darted ahead.
Lucy:	I suppose it could have been a trick, but Lizzie decided she couldn't just leave her there.
Bert:	What, and risk not winning the race she had trained so hard for?
Lucy:	Yeah! Incredible! She gave up the race to help her main rival. And guess what!
Bert:	What?
Lucy:	Tina Turbo wasn't messing about. She'd actually been knocked out. She could have drowned.

Bert:	Drowned?!
Lucy:	She was lying with her face in a puddle.
Bert:	Wow!
Lucy:	Lizzie Long pulled Tina Turbo to safety and then sat with her until the teacher came to help.
Bert:	Didn't any of the other runners help?
Lucy:	No, they were all trying too hard to win the race.
Bert:	That's a fantastic story. I reckon Lizzie Long is the true champion!
Lucy:	Bert, for once I agree with you!
Bert:	Hey! Watch it! We'd better go! Bye!
Lucy:	Yeah, bye!

Day Four: Determination

Bert:	Oh, I ache all over.
Lucy:	I'm not surprised. When you said you were going to go in the fun run, I laughed. I thought, there's no way he'll be able to run for six miles.
Bert:	It was seven miles!
Lucy:	Let's face it, Bert, the only running you normally do is running out of pocket money.
Bert:	Cheek! But when I heard that you could get people to sponsor you…
Lucy:	(Interrupts) What do you mean?
Bert:	People give you money for each mile you run.
Lucy:	Wow! Sounds like a great idea!
Bert:	Then you give that money away.
Lucy:	Doesn't sound like such a good idea.
Bert:	I decided I'd collect money for the Toybox Charity. They help homeless children.
Lucy:	I know. But seriously, Bert, I didn't think you could run that far.
Bert:	Neither did my mate, Tom. He laughed when I asked him to sponsor me, especially when I said it was seven miles. He said, 'I'll give you ten quid if you finish the race!'
Lucy:	Wow, that's very generous of him!
Bert:	That's what I said. But he said, 'No not really, I only said it because I know you've got no chance!'
Lucy:	That's not very nice.
Bert:	Yeah, it made me more determined than ever. I started to do some secret training.
Lucy:	Wow, sounds exciting!
Bert:	Then Tom found out and started to get worried. When the day of the race came, I was running along when Tom came running up to me and asked me if I wanted to have a go on his brand new PlayStation 2.
Lucy:	Wow, he's got one of those?
Bert:	I almost fell for it. I almost left the race. But then I realized that he was trying to distract me off course, so I kept going.

Lucy:	Good for you!
Bert:	After three miles, I was shattered. Tom came riding up to me and asked me if I wanted to jump on the back of his bike.
Lucy:	That was kind of him!
Bert:	No it wasn't! I knew, if I did that, it would have been cheating. So I told him to go away. He did—for a mile or two!
Lucy:	Good!
Bert:	Then he came back. He told me he had been chatting to Polly Perfect.
Lucy:	(In a jealous tone) Oh, her!
Bert:	He told me that she fancied me and wanted to see me straight away. Wow, my heart started pumping twice as fast!
Lucy:	Why?
Bert:	What do you mean, 'why'? She's such a babe! Once again, I almost left the race. Then I realized. He was trying to trick me again. Why would a gorgeous babe like her fancy me?
Lucy:	I do!
Bert:	What did you say?
Lucy:	Oh, nothing!
Bert::	All his tricks and his lies made me more determined than ever! And guess what, Lucy!
Lucy:	What?
Bert:	I made it! I was third from last, but that didn't matter. I made it! It was worth it in the end!

Lucy:	Well done! My hero! (She gives Bert a kiss)
Bert:	Yuck! What did you do that for? I'll have to wash my face now! Bye, everyone!
Lucy:	What do you mean, wash your face? Come back here, you cheeky Bert! (To audience) Oh, bye, everyone!

Reproduced with permission from *Champions!* published by BRF 2004 (1 84101 185 1)

Day Five: Decoration

Lucy: *(To audience)* Bert is a little bit late—he's still aching after his fun run. Ah, here he comes now. Let's all say, 'Ah! Poor Bert' when he arrives.

Bert comes in.

Lucy: *(And audience)* Ah! Poor Bert!

Bert: Ha, ha, very funny! It was worth it in the end, though. Look. *(Shows a medal round his neck)* Don't you think that's just great? *(Lucy encourages audience to give Bert a clap. Lucy gives him a kiss)*

Bert: Stop it!

Lucy: My hero!

Bert: Don't start that again!

Lucy: OK, my hero, I won't!

Bert: Hey! Anyway, I'm not the real hero. Lizzie Long is.

Lucy: Oh yeah! I saw her on telly.

Bert: *(To audience)* Our friend, Lizzie Long, didn't only run in the cross-country, she also ran in the fun run and she was the fastest under-11, so she got a special cup.

Lucy: Yeah! Not only that, but the local newspaper heard about how she had saved Tina Turbo.

Bert: And given up the chance of winning the race.

Lucy: So her photo was on the front page of the paper.

Bert: Then the local TV station heard about it and she ended up being interviewed and given a special badge for helping Tina. The headline was 'A true sportsperson!'

Lucy: Hey, I bet the Queen will invite her down to the palace for a nice cup of tea!

Bert: They might give her a special honour. Dame Lizzie Long!

Lucy: Our friend Lizzie will be well and truly decorated.

Bert: Yeah! And she will have deserved it.

Both: Our hero!

Lucy: I'm going to see if I can get her autograph.

Bert: Great idea. Wait for me!

Both: Bye!

Quick quiz questions

In each group, question number one is for the youngest group. Number two is for the middle group and number three is for the oldest group.

Day One: Direction

Odd one out?

1. Barbie, Action Man, the Prime Minister, Polly Pocket?
   (Prime Minister)
2. Apple, orange, burger, banana?
   (Burger)
3. Long jump, javelin, high jump, pole vault?
   (Javelin)

General Bible questions

1. What did Noah build? An aeroplane, a submarine or an ark?
   (Ark)
2. What was Daniel thrown into? A den of wolves, lions or bears?
   (Lions)
3. What was Joseph given by his dad? A coat, a hat or a pair of gloves?
   (Coat)

Watt family questions

1. What are the names of the boy and girl?
   (Rick and Wendy)
2. Grandma won a competition. What was the prize?
   (To go to the Olympic games)
3. What happened to Rick's super-soaker
   (Grandma Watt lost it)

Day Two: Distraction

Watt family questions

1. On the flight to the Olympic games, what did Grandma do that was embarrassing?
   (Keep-fit)
2. Why was the British coach upset?
   (Some of the top athletes had been kidnapped)
3. Who had kidnapped the athletes?
   (Mr Steel)

Bert and Lucy questions

1. In yesterday's puppet sketch, why was Lucy disqualified from the cross-country race?
   (She ran the wrong way round the course)
2. What was yesterday's memory verse?
   (Let us run with determination the race that lies before us)
3. Where can yesterday's memory verse be found in the Bible?
   (Hebrews 12:1–2)

1. Where did Jesus go in yesterday's Bible story?
   (*To the temple in Jerusalem*)
2. Why were Mary and Joseph upset?
   (*They couldn't find Jesus*)
3. What was he doing in the temple?
   (*He was chatting to the teachers*)

Day Three: Dedication

Up-front presentation questions

1. In today's puppet sketch, why was Lizzie Long a hero?
   (*Because she helped Tina Turbo*)
2. What disguise did Wendy Watt suggest their top athlete should use?
   (*Grey wig, skirt and walking-stick*)
3. But now what is happening to Grandma Watt?
   (*She's being chased by the baddie*)

Memory verse questions

If necessary, sing the first couple of words to remind the children of the songs.

1. Sing yesterday's memory verse together as a team.
   (*Keep yourself in training for a godly life*)
2. Sing the first day's memory verse together as a team.
   (*Let us run with determination the race that lies before us*)
3. Sing today's memory verse together as a team.
   (*Encourage one another and help one another*)

Bible story questions

1. In yesterday's Bible story, where did Jesus go to be alone with God?
   (*The desert*)
2. Who came to Jesus after he had been in the desert for 40 days?
   (*The devil*)
3. The devil tried to tempt Jesus to do wrong, but Jesus resisted. What did the devil try to get Jesus to do?
   (*Turn stones into bread, jump off the temple, bow down to him*)

Day Four: Determination

Up-front presentation questions

1. In today's puppet sketch, Bert took part in a fun run, but his mate Tom tried to distract him. How did Tom do this?
   (*Invited Bert to play on his PlayStation 2, offered him a ride on the back of his bike, told him that Polly Perfect fancied him*)
2. What was Mr Steel willing to exchange for the super athlete, Grandma Watt?
   (*The two athletes*)
3. Grandma wasn't prepared to do the swap because it was too dangerous, but who was prepared to take the risk in her place?
   (*Rick Watt*)

Memory verse questions

1. Ask for a volunteer to stand up and recite a memory verse.
2. Ask for another volunteer from a different team to recite a different memory verse.
3. Ask a volunteer from another team to recite a different memory verse.

Bible story questions

1. What was wrong with the man who was ill in yesterday's Bible story?
   (*He couldn't move his body*)
2. The four friends were dedicated to their friend and determined to get him to Jesus. Why?
   (*Because they believed that Jesus could heal him*)
3. Jesus did heal the man, and he was very impressed with the four friends. What impressed him?
   (*Their faith and their dedication*)

Day Five: Decoration

1. In today's puppet sketch, who was decorated and declared a true sportsperson?
   (Lizzie Long)
2. In the Watt family drama, who came to Rick's rescue?
   (Grandma and Wendy)
3. The athletes both won medals, but who were the real champions?
   (The Watt family)

Memory verse questions

1. As a team, sing a memory verse.
2. As a team, sing a different memory verse.
3. As a team, sing another memory verse.

Bible story questions

1. Why did some people want to get rid of Jesus in yesterday's Bible story?
   (Because they were jealous of him)
2. What happened to Jesus three days after he was put to death on the cross?
   (Jesus came back to life again)
3. Why did Jesus allow himself to be punished, even though he had done nothing wrong?
   (Because he loves us and wants us to be forgiven for the things we do wrong. Jesus wants us to be part of his family)

Bible narrations

Day One: Direction

Champion athletes don't become champions overnight. Many begin their sport when they are children. There's a lot to learn, many experiences to go through and plenty of hard work. A combination of these factors will go towards producing a champion athlete. Sometimes we might think that God could have saved time by planning for Jesus to arrive on earth as an adult, but the route that he chose—for Jesus to be born as a baby—meant that Jesus was able to experience life as we experience it, with plenty of time to learn and prepare for the work that God had for him to do.

Read Luke 2:41–52 (the boy Jesus in the temple).

> **Cast**
> Narrator and two others (A and B)

A: I love watching the Olympics (or athletics) on telly—all those super-fit athletes. They're a bit like me, really!

B: Ha! In your dreams. Those athletes often begin when they're children and train hard for years. There is so much to learn and they have to be super-fit!

A: OK, I get your point!

Narr: That's like God.

A+B: What is?

Narr: He started young. In fact, he started as a baby.

A+B: A baby?

Narr: Just imagine for a second that you were God and you were really upset because people had messed up your world. You had put them in charge—you'd wanted them to be like 'caretakers' but instead they had just become 'takers'. They were greedy and selfish, stealing and killing one another. What would you do?

A: Easy! I would show the whole world my great power! I would suddenly appear in the sky and, in a big booming voice, declare *(in a powerful voice)* 'Stop being mean to one another and turn back to me! Or else!'

B: *(Jumps out of skin)* Gosh! That scared me! That's really telling them!

Narr: Yes, it would scare everyone! God wants people to obey and love him—but not because they are terrified of him!

A+B: What did God do, then?

Narr: He chose to become one of us. The Son of God!

A: Wow! I bet he had real power. A superhero! Imagine being a boy but really being God in disguise. You could cheat in all the games. You wouldn't have to run in 'tag'—you'd hover above the ground or just appear behind someone. 'Boo!' It would be great!

B: Imagine playing 'I Spy'. You'd know the answers straight away. Awesome!

Narr: No, you've got it wrong! God's Son did have an amazing birth, with angels singing in the sky and a star guiding the way. He was 'Emmanuel—God with us!' But Jesus didn't come just to show off. He came to save the world. He showed people how to live without cheating. And he wasn't God in disguise. In fact, he was just a normal boy. He was fully human and fully God. But he never used his power until he was older, and then never for himself but to help others.

A: Do we know anything about him as a boy?

Narr: Yes, there is one story. Jesus was twelve and he and his family were going on a sort of holiday—off to the city of Jerusalem to celebrate the Passover feast.

B:	The Passover? I've heard of that. That's when the Jews remember how God rescued them from slavery in Egypt.
A:	*(To B)* Gosh! You never cease to amaze me!
Narr:	And as a twelve-year-old boy, that would have been a very special age. Your parents would almost certainly have taken you to Jerusalem so you could take part in the celebrations!
A:	Wow! Sounds exciting!
B:	Sounds like a long journey to me!

Narr:	It was. But lots of people travelled together and the journey was all part of the holiday! There were children playing games, swimming and cooling off in the Jordan, passing through great cities like Jericho!
A:	Wow! Sounds great!
Narr:	Then, there in front of you, you'd have seen Jerusalem with its magnificent temple. Inside, there were many religious teachers telling the stories about how God set them free. Then there was a huge feast.
B:	Wow, they must have had a great time!
Narr:	Yep! But all good things must come to an end. All the people who travelled from Nazareth would have journeyed back together. But that's when they realized…!
A:	What?
Narr:	He was missing!
B:	Who?
Narr:	Mary and Joseph's son!
A+B:	Jesus!
Narr:	They thought he'd been playing with the others, but he hadn't been. He was missing. *Panic!*
A:	What? No need to panic! After all, Jesus was the Son of God.
B:	Yes, that was what the angels had said— 'Emmanuel, God with us!'

Narr:	Yes, but it was easy for his parents to forget who he really was. To them, he was their little boy, lost and alone in Jerusalem. They searched for days. Then suddenly…
A:	*(In a posh voice)* Let's go and hear that new religious teacher.
B:	Yes, he's amazing and he's only twelve!
Narr:	Could it be? Yes, it was their son, Jesus. He was chatting to all the religious teachers, and they were amazed! Jesus seemed to know God—and the scriptures—so well.
A:	Of course he did!
B:	He wrote the book!
Narr:	Jesus' parents gave him a bit of a telling off for making them so worried.
A:	But why? Had they forgotten who Jesus was? The Son of God!
B:	*(To A)* We've already been through that! They didn't understand!
Narr:	Jesus explained how he had to be in his father's house.
A:	He meant his heavenly father—God.
Narr:	He wanted to be close to God and discover what he wanted him to do.
B:	I bet his parents still struggled to understand.
Narr:	Well, it can't have been easy. For the time being, Jesus needed to live with his parents and carry on learning Joseph's trade—being a carpenter. He had to obey them. This was all part of his training, helping him to get ready for the work that God had for him to do.
All:	And Jesus grew both in body and in wisdom, gaining favour with God and people.

Day Two: Distraction

Jesus was tired. He'd been in the desert for forty days when the devil came to him, trying to tempt him off course by encouraging him to cheat. It's easy to give in to temptation when you are tired.

Read Matthew 4:1–12 (the temptation of Jesus).

> ### Cast
> Narrator and two others (A and B)

Narr:	*(To audience)* I wonder how you behave when you're tired. *(Name of A)* can be very silly!

A comes on yawning, spots the audience, pulls a very silly grin and does a silly wave.

A:	Hello, everyone, it's me!
Narr:	*(To audience)* See what I mean? Whereas *(name of B)* tends to be grumpy and cross!
B:	*(Yawning—then in a grumpy, cross voice)* I'm never grumpy and cross!
Narr:	*(To audience)* See what I mean? It's also easy, when you are tired, to be tempted to do things that are wrong.
A:	Imagine what it's like when you're a tired athlete.
B:	Yeah, you might be tempted to *cheat*!
Narr:	Exactly. And to make things worse, in any race there is the other team—the opposition— and sometimes the opposition may be mean to you and say something like this…
A:	*(Talking to B about the Narrator so that s/he can hear)* Well, I was really worried about the race until I saw the opposition, but look at him/her, s/he's a right weed!
B:	Yeah, I bet you could blow him/her over with one breath!

Narr:	Or they may try to bribe you by offering you a reward if you will let them win.
A:	*(To narrator)* Here, I'll give you ten quid if you pretend to fall over during the race!
B:	Yep, you may as well accept the ten quid, 'cos you've got no chance of winning the race. *(Talking about A)* S/he's never been beaten!
Narr:	Or they may try to put you off by making you feel so small that you lose all your confidence, and then they win. That's exactly what happened to Jesus. Jesus was now a grown-up man and ready to do the work God had for him. He needed to prepare, as it were, for the race. So he went into the desert to be alone with God.

A:	What, like an athlete's training camp?
Narr:	Er, yes, why not? He went to find out what God wanted him to do. He was there for 40 days and nights with no food, so he must have been very hungry and tired.
A:	Very tired.
B:	In fact, very, very tired.
Narr:	Suddenly the opposition turned up in the form of the devil. He'd come along to try to make Jesus feel small, or even to persuade him to cheat.

A stands mid-stage looking forward. B stands to the side of A and looks at him, then talks to him—moving behind him, then back again, like an interrogator. A watches and listens to B.

B:	*(To A)* So you are Jesus, the Son of God, are you? You must be hungry! Why don't you turn these stones into bread and eat your fill? After all, that should be no problem for someone like you.
Narr:	But that's not God's way, and anyway he's not going to let the devil tell him what to do. So Jesus said…
A:	The scripture says, 'Human beings cannot live by bread alone, but need every word that God speaks.'
B:	*(To narrator)* What does he mean by that?
Narr:	Food's good.
B:	Yep!
Narr:	But listening to God and obeying him is better.
B:	Right! I'll try another one!
Narr:	The devil whisked Jesus away. Suddenly he was standing on top of the temple in Jerusalem, looking down.
B:	It's a long way down. Jump! Go on! God won't let anything happen to you. His angels will catch you. You won't even scratch your foot.
Narr:	Wow, if the people below saw that, they'd immediately see that Jesus was the Son of God! But it wasn't in God's plan. And Jesus said…
A:	Do not put the Lord your God to the test!
B:	*(Sarcastically)* Sorry. It was only an idea.
Narr:	So once again the devil whisked Jesus away— this time to the top of a high mountain where Jesus could see many great cities and kingdoms.
B:	*(Sarcastically)* Now, you know me—I'm true to my word! I'll give you all this… if you bow down and worship me. So what do you say?
Narr:	Who does he think he is? That's not God's way! So Jesus said…
A:	Go away, Satan! The scripture says, 'Worship the Lord your God and serve only him.'
B:	I give up!

Narr:	Then Satan left Jesus. Even though he was tired and hungry, Jesus proved that he was still strong. He wasn't going to cheat or take the easy option, he was going to obey God and follow his plan for the race.
A:	*(To audience)* So when you are tired, be extra careful not to be tempted to do wrong!
B:	But be like Jesus, be strong and do what is right and don't let yourself—and God—down.

Day Three: Dedication

Not only did Jesus spend time with God, just as an athlete would spend time with his coach, but he also chose a team to help him in the work God had called him to. Jesus trained, encouraged and looked after his team. Then, one day, he met another team by whom he was very impressed!

Read Mark 2:1–12 (Jesus heals a paralysed man).

> ### Cast
> Narrator and two others (A and B)

A:	*(Comes on jogging and trying to look sporty)* I had a dream last night. I dreamt that I won the World Cup. But the amazing thing was, I didn't have a team. I was so fast, so skilful, so fit, so cool, that I won all on my own. I'm simply the best! *(To B)* Do you think that dream might come true?
B:	Of course not! You would need a very dedicated coach to train you. And win on your own? I don't think so! You would need a brilliant team in order to stand a chance in the World Cup.
Narr:	Jesus had a very difficult race ahead—an impossible task—to bring people who had forgotten God back to him. He chose a team to help him. They were very ordinary to begin with, but with Jesus' training they became extraordinary people.
A:	Wow!
B:	Cool!
Narr:	But today's story isn't about that team. It's about another team who really impressed Jesus. They were a group of mates.
A+B:	Like us!
Narr:	They would have had a laugh together.
A+B:	Like us!
Narr:	Pulled each other's legs. *(A pulls B's leg)*
B:	He doesn't mean like that! He means like this!

	(B points up in the air) What's that?
A:	*(A looks up)* What?
B:	Nothing. I was just pulling your leg! *(A looks confused)*
Narr:	Exactly. They had fun together. But one of the mates didn't join in.
A:	Spoilsport!
Narr:	No, not at all. He couldn't join in. But his mates didn't mind, they were very kind to him. Every day they would carry him outside and put him on the side of the road!

B:	You call that kind? I call that strange!
Narr:	No, you don't understand. He was paralysed. He couldn't walk or even move his arms. This meant that he couldn't work, so his friends would carry him outside every day and, hopefully, people would give him food or money to help him survive.
A:	Great mates!
Narr:	But today, things were going to be different.
A:	*(To B)* Here, I've heard that Jesus is in town and I've heard that Jesus can make people better.
B:	Are you thinking what I think you're thinking?
A:	I sure am! Maybe he can heal our mate!
B:	Yes, but there are going to be lots of people trying to see Jesus.
A:	Yes, but we've got to try!
B:	He's a heavy lump!
A:	He sure is, but we've got to try!
B:	It's a hot, sweaty day! What if Jesus can't heal him?
A:	What if he can? We've got to try!
Narr:	So they did try—all four of them.
B:	Here, there's only two of us!

Reproduced with permission from *Champions!* published by BRF 2004 (1 84101 185 1)

Narr: Go and get some volunteers, then. Two for the back and one to be carried!

A and B fetch three volunteers from the audience, one to be carried and the other two helping A and B to carry him/her, with one mate at each arm and leg.

A: Cor, he is a lump!

B: Let's go, guys. *(They start to walk around the stage)*

Narr: It would have been a hot day.

A: It's a hot day!

Narr: It may have been a long way.

B: It's a long way!

Narr: But they finally arrived. They could see the house that Jesus was in, but there was a large crowd blocking the way.

A: What are we going to do?

B: Go home.

A: No way!

Narr: So they carefully pushed their way through the crowd.

Prime some leaders to come out and form a crowd. The group of mates push their way through, treading on some toes on the way.

Narr: Finally, they made it to the house, but everyone was trying to get in through the door or look in at the windows. There was no way through!

A: What are we going to do?

B: Go home.

A: No way!

Narr: *(Team mime as narrator speaks)* They went round the house to some narrow steps that led up to the house's flat roof.

B: What, up those narrow, steep steps?

A: Yep!

B: My arms are dropping off!

A: Made it.

B: There's no door or chimney. What now?

A: Put him down, guys, and let's make a hole.

B: A hole?

A: Come on, we're so close, we can't give up now!

B: Yeah! *(They mime making a hole in the roof)*

Narr: That's exactly what they did. They were so determined to get their mate to Jesus, they would stop at nothing. They knew that Jesus could change their friend's life for ever, and that's exactly what happened.

A: Yeah, we lowered him down, right at Jesus' feet.

B: Jesus said to our mate, 'Your sins are forgiven!'

A: The crowd was not impressed, but then Jesus proved that he had the right to forgive sins.

B: 'Cos he said to our mate, 'Get up! Take up your bed and walk!' And guess what?

All: He did!

Narrator asks the one who had been carried to get up, walk, jump and dance.

Narr: They were all so happy, everyone praised God.

A: Jesus was impressed by our faith…

B: …and how we cared for our friend.

A: But we were so impressed by Jesus because he changed our friend's life for the better. Wouldn't it be great if we were all that dedicated to our friends?

B: Wouldn't it be great if we were all determined to introduce our friends to Jesus?

Narr: Yeah. For a start, we could invite them along to 'Champions'! If we don't want our friends to miss out, we all need some…

All: DEDICATION!

Day Four: Determination

In a race such as a marathon, the athletes will become very tired and even start to experience some pain. If they carry on running, they may go through what is known as the pain barrier, but they need to push on if they are to finish the race and receive the prize. Jesus knew when the time had come near for him to leave the world and return to his heavenly father. He also knew that he was to suffer the pain of the cross and that he must push on through the 'pain barrier' and finish the race.

Read Mark 15 and 16; John 20:1–23 (Jesus' death and resurrection).

> ## Cast
> Narrator and two others (A and B)

Narr: *(To A)* Have you ever considered running a marathon?

A: What, me, run 26 miles? Only if *(name of B)* would carry me when I got tired!

B: Ha! What, a lump like you? *(Sarcastically)* Of course I would carry you. After all, you are my friend!

Narr: You don't just get tired. People actually go through the pain barrier.

A: Pain! Hey, *(name of B)*, would you carry the pain for me, too?

B: Did you say pain? No, sorry, I don't like pain! It hurts! *(To A)* If you chose to run in a marathon and suffered pain, then you'd only have yourself to blame. Besides, no one can take on your pain for you!

Narr: That reminds me of what Jesus did for us. A lot of people thought that Jesus was wonderful.

A: I think Jesus is great! *(Thumbs up)*

Narr: But other people hated him.

B: They hated him! *(Thumbs down)*

A: Why did they hate him?

Narr: Well, Jesus was a really interesting guy. He told stories about God and people travelled for miles to listen to him. You see, suddenly it all made sense, and they started to understand that God actually loved them and that he wanted them to love him too.

A: Excellent!

Narr: But some people—those whose job it was to teach people about God—often just ended up confusing people. They weren't great storytellers like Jesus, and it never occurred to them to tell people that God loved them, so they didn't have crowds flocking to see them. They became jealous of Jesus.

B: We've gotta get rid of him—he's far too popular! Let's tell lies about him so that he gets arrested and sentenced to death!

A: That won't work. Jesus is far too clever. We won't stand a chance.

Narr: That's true. Jesus could have called down thousands of angels from heaven and the religious leaders who were plotting against him wouldn't have stood a chance.

A: *(Chants)* Excellent! Go Jesus, go, go, go! Will they beat him? No, no, no!

Narr: But he didn't!

A: *(Excitedly)* What? He didn't call down thousands of angels?

Narr: No, he let the temple guards arrest him instead.

A: What?

Narr: Yes, they arrested him, found him guilty of causing trouble and sentenced him to death. In those days, that meant being nailed to a cross. So they did just that—they nailed him to a cross and watched him die.

B: At last! That's the end of him!

A: No, no, no! That can't be right! No way!

Narr: *(Name of B)* is right. Jesus let them kill him. It was all part of God's plan. They put him to death by nailing him to a cross.

A: But why?

Narr: That's exactly what Jesus' friends wanted to know. They were so upset. Some of them watched Jesus die. Others ran away. Afterwards, many of them hid in a house together.

A: This is such a sad story.

Narr: Well, yes and no! You see, three days later, all Jesus' friends were hiding in the house when suddenly Mary knocked on the door, and said…

B: I've seen him! He's alive.

A: Seen who? Who's alive?

B: Jesus!

A: Jesus? No, Jesus is dead.

B: I know he was, but not any more! He's alive again!

Narr: They all thought she had gone mad, but late on that Sunday evening, guess who suddenly appeared in the room?

A: Who?

B: Jesus! They could see that he wasn't a ghost. It was really him! He had come back to life again!

Narr: Yes, he had won! He was victorious! He'd conquered death! Alive for ever!

A: *(Excitedly)* Hurray! Go Jesus, go, go, go! But I still don't understand. What's all this about?

Narr: Listen, imagine you were running a marathon and you became tired. Imagine you were going through the pain barrier. Wouldn't it be wonderful if someone came along, picked you up and took on your pain?

B: Ha! No one would do that. No one can take on your pain!

A: That's right! Anyway, what has that got to do with it? I still don't understand.

Narr: Well, Jesus died on the cross because he loves us! It's as if he's taken on the pain of our being separated from God by all the things we do wrong. He's taken the blame in our place. So, because of what Jesus did for us, we can be with God for ever.

A little rhyme:

Narr: He took the pain. He took the blame.
B: For the wrong things that we do.
Narr: He paid the price, the sacrifice.
A: He died for me and you!

Narr: So now we can be on God's side.
B: And be a part of his family.
A: So thank you, Jesus, for all you do.
All: And thank you for loving me.

Day Five: Decoration

When a champion wins the race, he or she climbs on to the podium for all to see, and receives the medal for finishing the race. So it was with Jesus. Jesus had run the race and stayed on course. He has won the race. Jesus is the ultimate champion. A short while after his resurrection, Jesus met with his disciples. He led them out of the city of Jerusalem as far as Bethany, where he raised his hands and blessed them. While he was blessing them, he was lifted up to heaven to take his place as the King of kings and Lord of lords.

Read Luke 24:50–53 and Acts 1:1–11 (Jesus is taken up to heaven and is exalted to the highest place—alive and victorious).

> ### Cast
> Narrator and two others (A and B)

Narr: Did you know that when the leading runner in a marathon enters the stadium, all the other events stop and everyone in the stadium cheers, as the champion completes the last lap? *(Runner comes in, people Ch)*

A: Wow! That must be so exciting. What an atmosphere!

B: Yes, after 26 miles of solid running, that must really spur them on for the last lap.

Narr: Then, finally, the champion climbs on to the podium to receive their medal. They've done it! *(Runner climbs on podium and has medal put round neck)*

A: A very proud moment!

B: And everyone honours them for their fantastic achievement. *(Hold up Clap Si)*

Narr: It was like this with Jesus. He had finished the race and completed everything that God had asked him to do.

A: What was that, then?

B: I know! He was kind to people and wanted everyone to know how special they are.

Narr: Yep! And he wants us to be kind to others too. What else?

A: I know! He told stories about what God is like. No one is as great and powerful as God.

B: *(Interrupts)* But he still loves us and wants us to love him, too.

A: *(Slightly cross with B for interrupting)* Hey, I was about to say that!

Narr: Then comes the hard bit.

A: When he died on the cross, he took the blame for all the wrong things we say and do.

B: Then he came back to life again! What a champion!

Narr: You can say that again!

B: What a champion!

Narr: Exactly! About 40 days after he had risen from the dead, Jesus and his friends went to the hill outside the city of Jerusalem called the Mount of Olives. He was going to say goodbye.

A: Where was he off to, then?

Narr: It was time for him to return to heaven. As he was talking to them, he seemed be getting taller! *(Look up)*

A: *(Pretends to watch Jesus going up, and says to B)* Is he getting taller? *(look up)*

B: *(Pretends to notice Jesus' feet leaving the ground)* Hey, look, his feet aren't touching the ground! *(Point to ground)*

A: Don't be silly. *(Looks down, too)* Gosh, you're right, he's rising up! *(A and B (open-mouthed) gradually look higher and higher) (look up)*

Narr: They watched Jesus rising higher and higher… *(Both A and B do a little (wave,) then look at each other.) Both look totally amazed and (look up again)* … until finally he disappeared into the clouds. Suddenly, two

(still looking up).

men dressed in white appeared from nowhere and said… *(A and B still looking up. Narrator speaks in a loud voice, startling both A and B and making them jump)* 'Men of Galilee!' *(Jump)*

A: Here, you made us jump!

B: Where did you guys suddenly appear from?

Narr: 'Why are you looking up into the sky?' they said. 'Jesus has gone back to heaven, but one day he'll come back again.'

B: Who were they?

Narr: They were angels and they were basically saying that Jesus had finished his work and gone to heaven to take his place as the King of kings and Lord of lords!

A: Like a champion athlete climbing on to the podium to receive his prize.

B: Yes, Jesus was the ultimate champion!

Narr: Jesus still is the ultimate champion.

All: And he shall reign for ever and ever. Amen.

49

Day One: Direction

Shade in the shapes with a dot to find the hidden message

Help the athlete find the right path!

Start

There are eight differences between these two pictures. See if you can find them all.

Day One: Direction

Find the words hidden in the grid.

| boy |
| Jesus |
| temple |
| twelve |
| years |
| old |
| Jerusalem |
| amazed |
| parents |
| teachers |
| obedient |
| wisdom |

T	W	I	S	D	O	M	A	R	K
E	E	B	O	E	B	L	V	J	I
M	B	A	Z	Y	E	A	D	E	N
P	T	O	C	A	D	J	O	S	D
L	W	T	Y	H	I	H	N	U	D
E	P	P	A	R	E	N	T	S	E
Y	E	A	R	S	N	R	O	V	Z
E	V	L	E	W	T	L	S	E	A
R	J	E	R	U	S	A	L	E	M
C	H	A	M	P	I	O	N	S	A

Find the hidden message

Code: 1 = a; 2 = e; 3 = i; 4 = o; 5 = u

l _2_ t   _5_ s   r _5_ n   w _3_ t h   d _2_ t _2_ r m _3_ n _1_ t _3_ _4_ n   t h _2_

r _1_ c _2_   t h _1_ t   l _3_ _2_ s   b _2_ f _4_ r _2_   _5_ s .   l _2_ t   _5_ s

k _2_ _2_ p   _4_ _5_ r   _2_ y _2_ s   f _3_ x _2_ d   _4_ n   J _2_ s _5_ s   _4_ n

w h _4_ m   _4_ _5_ r   f _1_ _3_ t h   d _2_ p _2_ n d s .

(H _2_ b r _2_ w s   1 2 : 1 – 2)

Day Two: Distraction

Colour in the things that might distract the athlete.

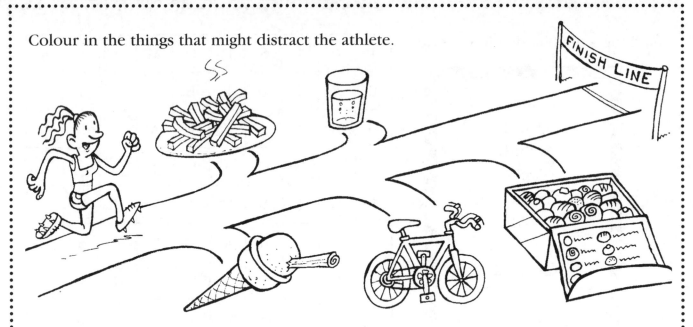

How many stones can you see in the picture and how many loaves of bread?

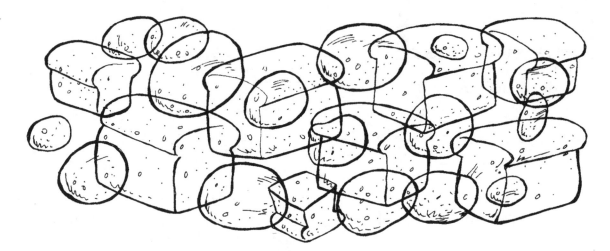

Be a champion! Help the athlete find the way by colouring in the track.

Day Two: Distraction

Spot ten differences between the two pictures.

Fill in the words on the grid.

temptation
devil
cheat
distraction
champion
strong
faithful
son
of
God

Day Three: Dedication

Spot the differences between the two pictures. See how many you can find.

Put a cross through the bubbles that aren't encouraging and colour in the encouraging bubbles.

You did your best. Well done!

We don't want you in our team!

I could do better with my eyes closed!

Don't cry! You did well!

Come and join our team!

You're too slow to be a runner!

Wow! You're much better!

Cry baby!

You're useless!

Day Three: Dedication

Find the right track and reveal today's memory verse.

```
m o a n c h e a t s a n o t h e r s u n e a n o t h e r →
g r u m b l e r o n e b o s s y a b a t n f i g h t e r
→ e n c o u r a g e h u r t i n g n f u n o m i g h t y s
b e s t b y f a r b i g h e a r d h e l p g r e a t e r
```

(1 Thessalonians 5:11)

Join the dots to find out what happens to the athlete who is hurt.

Find the words in the wordsearch.

C	K	C	I	W	D	R	A	N
R	I	F	R	I	E	N	D	S
O	N	A	O	J	Z	A	Y	S
W	D	I	H	U	O	M	T	U
D	N	T	E	L	R	H	S	S
F	E	H	O	U	S	E	N	E
U	P	L	E	H	J	E	X	J
N	E	N	C	O	U	R	A	G
P	A	R	A	L	Y	S	E	D

paralysed   **Jesus**

man   **crowd**

faith   **house**

four   **help**

friends

Day Four: Determination

Colour in the letters with dots to find the Bible verse.

Romans 8:31

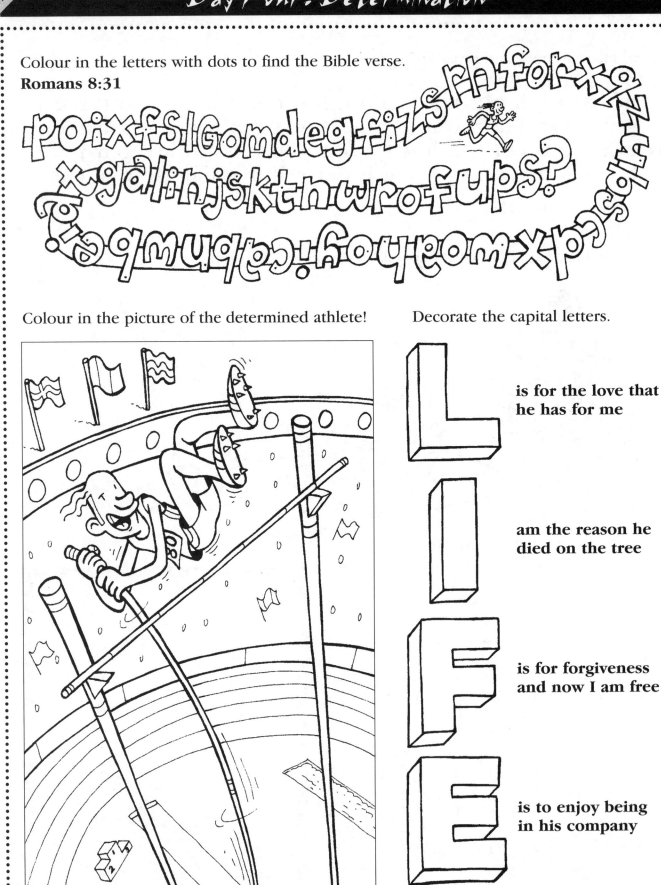

Colour in the picture of the determined athlete!

Decorate the capital letters.

L is for the love that he has for me

I am the reason he died on the tree

F is for forgiveness and now I am free

E is to enjoy being in his company

Day Four: Determination

Find the word.

1. He
2. suffered
3. pain
4. for
5. us
6. blame
7. died
8. love
9. forgiven

			H	E			
			L	S			
			U	O			
F	O	R	G	I	V	E	N
P	A	I	N	D	I	E	D
			Z	E			
			B	R			
			L	E			
			A	F			
			M	F			
			E	U			
			D	S			

Spot nine differences between the two pictures.

Help Mary to find the disciples so that she can tell them the good news that Jesus is alive!

Day Five: Decoration

Join the dots to see what the disciples are looking at, and then colour the picture.

Spot eight differences between the two pictures.

Colour in the Bible verse.

Philippians 3:14

Day Five: Decoration

Fit the words into the grid to find the hidden word.

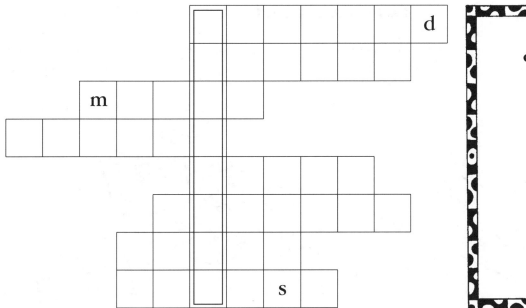

crowned

medal

prize

victory

podium

glory

heaven

finish

The ultimate champion! Colour in the clouds that describe the disciples' feelings when Jesus ascended to heaven.

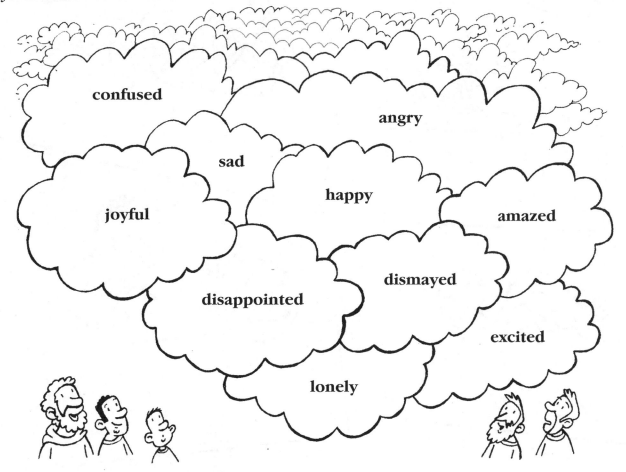

Reproduced with permission from *Champions!* published by BRF 2004 (1 84101 185 1)

Appendix One

Champions! badges

Use the templates below to make badges for the children. Photocopy on to thin card and attach a safety-pin to the back with a strip of masking tape. The children can colour in their own badges and write their names in the space. Younger children might need team leaders to help them write their names.

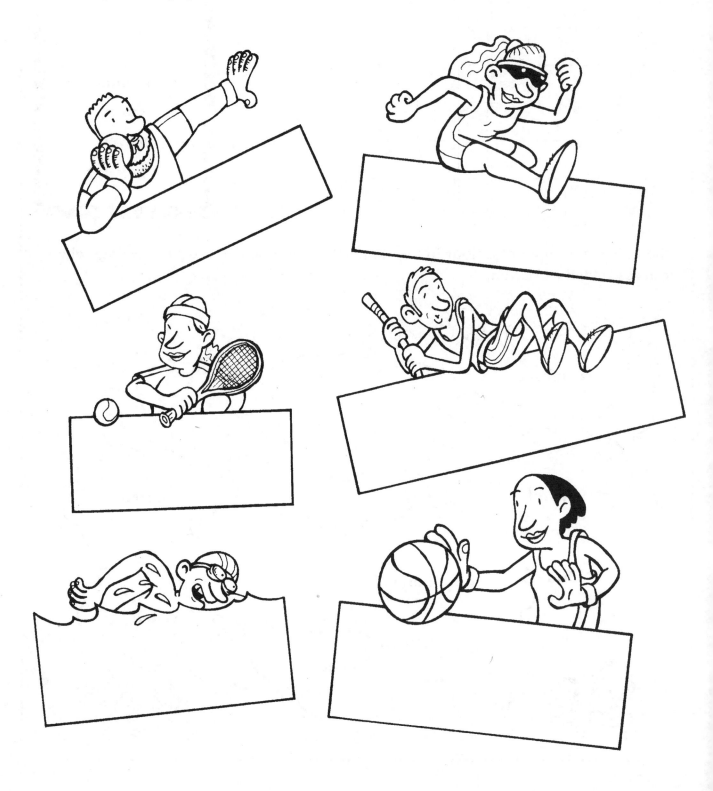

Appendix Two

Champions! invitation cards

Photocopy the template below to make invitation cards for the *Champions!* holiday club, and fill in your own contact number. The children can colour them in and give them out to their friends and classmates.

Champions! registration form

Champions!

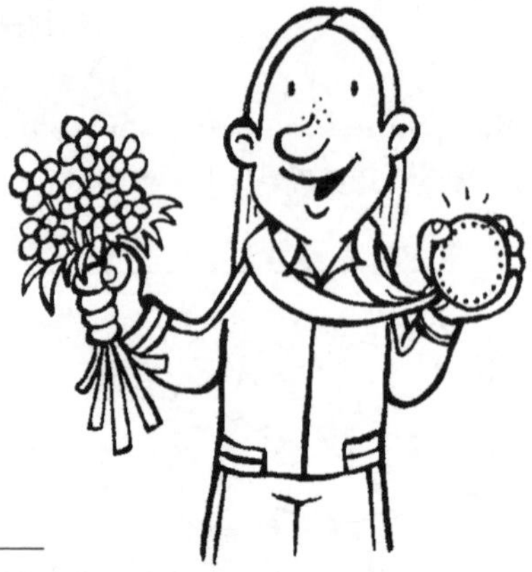

Name ______________________________

Address ______________________________

____

Date of birth ____________ Telephone number ______________________________

Contact in case of emergency ______________________________

Second contact in case of emergency ______________________________

Special needs, including allergies and medication ______________________________

____

School attended ______________________________

Church attended ______________________________

I hereby give permission for ____________________ (name of child) to take part in activities at ____________________ (name of venue), and my consent for medical treatment or first aid arising out of illness or accident.

Signed ______________________________ Date ____________

Parent/guardian

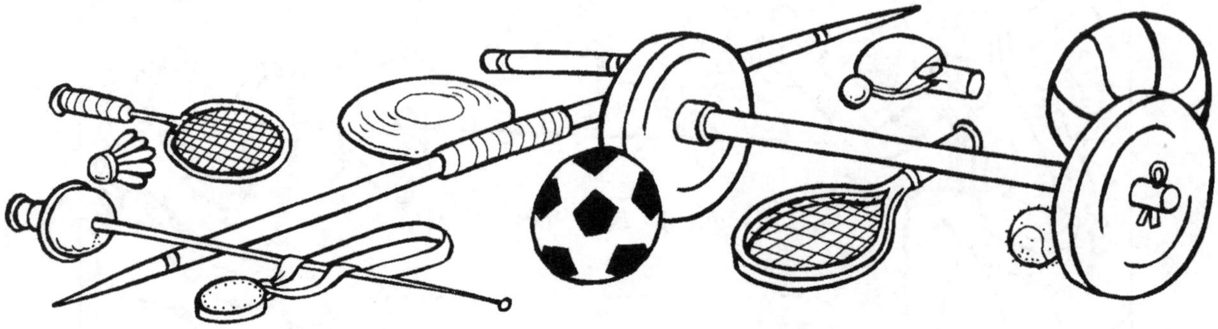

Champions! presentation poster

Use this poster to invite parents, relatives and friends to a *Champions!* event to find out what the children have been doing during their holiday club week.

Appendix Three

Decathlon board game

Spinner and counters

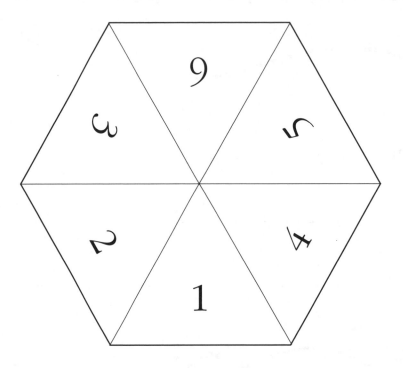

Decathlon board game template

36 WINNER!	**35** Threw the discus into crowd. Go back 6	**34**	**33**	**32** Personal best throw in the javelin. Go forward 2	**31**
25	**26**	**27** Twisted your ankle in the long jump. Go back 4	**28**	**29**	**30**
24 Came first in high jump. Go forward 2	**23**	**22**	**21** Ran 400 metres with the wind behind you. Go forward 3	**20**	**19**
13	**14** Lost the shot put. Go back 3	**15**	**16**	**17**	**18** Got stuck in mud during pole vault. Go back 2
12	**11**	**10**	**9** Came second in 100 metres. Go forward 4	**8**	**7**
START **1**	**2**	**3** Trip over a hurdle. Go back 2	**4**	**5**	**6**

Reproduced with permission from *Champions!* published by BRF 2004 (1 84101 185 1)

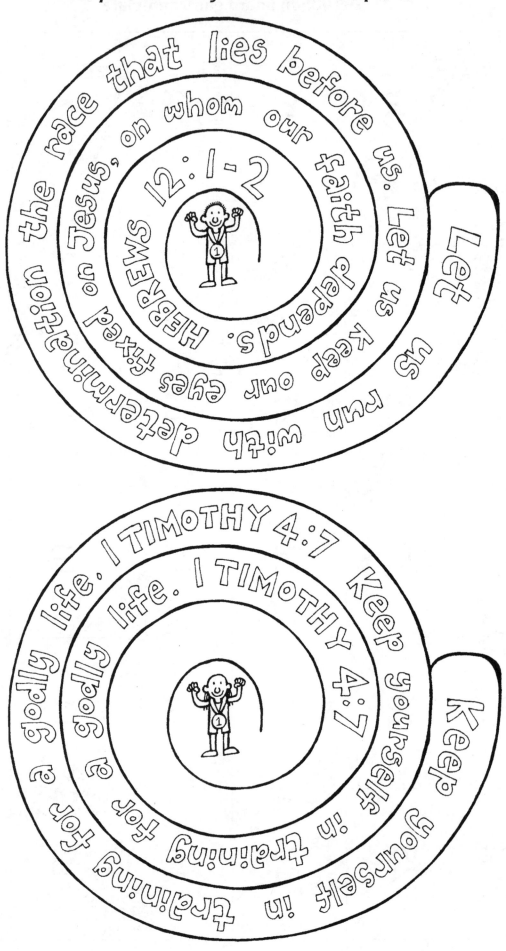

Encourage one another and help one another. I THESSALONIANS 5:11 Encourage one another and help one another. I THESSALONIANS 5:11

I'm gonna run straight towards the goal in order to win the prize – the prize that the LORD will give me on that day! 2 TIMOTHY 4:8 AND BASED ON PHILIPPIANS 3:14

Moving athlete card

Mini Olympics

All the games are played with the group split into teams. Each game is timed to last three minutes.

> **You will need:**
> • Five cones per team
> • One bucket per team
> • One football per team
> • One juggling ball per player
> • One parachute or sheet per team
> • One sack per team
> • One dessert spoon tied to a stick per team

Knock down!

Each player picks up the ball and zig-zags between the cones until they reach the line. The player then turns around and throws the ball between his or her legs, trying to knock over the bucket. The player collects the ball and hands it to the next player. The game is scored by the number of times the bucket has been knocked over by each team at the end of the time allowed.

In the bucket

The last player in the line goes to hold the bucket, ready to catch the ball thrown by the first player.

To start the game, the first player hops between the cones, then stops at the line and tries to throw the juggling ball into the bucket. If s/he misses, the ball stays on the ground. If the player succeeds, the ball remains in the bucket.

The bucket holder then runs to the back of the line,

and the first player takes over holding the bucket, ready to catch the second player's ball. The game continues until everyone has had a turn. The game is scored by the number of balls in the bucket at the end of the time allowed.

Obstacle course

The first player hops between the cones, crawls under the parachute or sheet, jumps in the sack to the finishing line and then runs back to tag the next player. The game is scored by the number of team members completing the course by the end of the time allowed.

Ball-and-spoon race

The first player takes the dessert spoon tied to a stick and zig-zags between the cones to the line, where a leader is waiting for them. The leader places a ball in the spoon. The player then carefully makes their way back with the ball and drops it into the bucket. If the player drops the ball before reaching the bucket, they cannot retrieve it.

When the player has completed the course, or after he or she has dropped the ball, the spoon is handed to the next player. The game is scored by the number of balls in the bucket at the end of the time allowed.

Ball-and-spoon relay

The first player is given a spoon with the ball already in place. On the word 'go', the first player runs to the line, around the cone and back to the second player. The second player carefully takes the spoon and ball from the first player and runs to the line, around the cone and back to the third player, who carefully takes the spoon and ball. The game continues until each player has completed the course.

If a player drops the ball, they can retrieve it by scooping the ball back on to the spoon without using their other hand. The game is scored by the number of team members completing the course at the end of the time allowed.

No hands, please!

The first player runs to the line, picks up a ball and puts it under his or her chin. S/he then hops back to the parachute or sheet, crawls underneath it, runs round the cones and drops the ball in the bucket. The game is scored by the number of balls in the bucket at the end of the time allowed.

Appendix Four

Time fillers

Quick activities

Design a logo

You might like to think about designing a logo for your team, or an overall logo for the *Champions!* holiday club. Your ideas might include:

- Different sports such as running, discus, boxing, hockey, tennis, fencing, football, weight lifting, swimming, golf, shot put and javelin
- Different items of equipment used by the athletes, such as running shoes, discus, boxing gloves, hockey stick, tennis racket, fencing foil, football, dumb-bells, swimming goggles, golf clubs, shorts, swimming costume and football boots
- Items of equipment used in the races, such as starting pistols, stopwatch or whistle
- Olympic flames
- Olympic rings
- Olympic medals
- National flags
- Your team name

Word busters

Give the children sheets of paper with a word or phrase written at the top. They have to see how many words they can make out of the key word, using each letter only once in each word, and not using plurals or proper nouns.

Suggested word list for younger children:
- Direction
- Distraction
- Dedication
- Determination
- Decoration

Suggested word list for older children:
- Jesus in the temple
- The temptation of Jesus
- The paralysed man
- Olympic games
- Marathon runner

Champions! bookmarks

Photocopy the template on to thin card to make *Champions!* bookmarks. The children can colour in their bookmark, write their name in the space and keep it as a souvenir of their holiday club fun.

This bookmark belongs to:

72

Quick games

Yes and no

Ask for a volunteer to be interviewed. They must answer the questions but are not allowed to say 'Yes' or 'No' or to repeat themselves (for example, by saying, 'maybe' over and over again). They are not allowed to hesitate either. See if they can last for a minute.

The interview could start something like this:

'What's your name?'
'Are you sure about that?'
'What's your favourite sport? I bet it's belly dancing.'
'What's your favourite food? I bet it's liver.'
'Sprouts?'
'Chips?'
'Are you married?'
'Would you like to be married?'
'Do you go to school?'
'Are you the headteacher?'
'Caretaker?'

Add as many questions as you need.

Friends

This game is based on the television programme *Mr and Mrs*. Choose two friends. One leaves the room. Ask the other one three questions, such as, 'What is your friend's least favourite subject at school?' or 'What is your friend's favourite pop group?' or 'How many brothers does your friend have?' and so on. Then ask the first friend to come back into the room. Ask him or her the same questions and see how well the friends know each other.

Fish and chips

This is a similar game to 'Yes and no'. Ask for a volunteer to be interviewed as before, but this time all they are allowed to say is 'fish and chips'.

The interview could start something like this:

'What's your name?' *(Reply)* 'Fish and chips.'
'What did you have for breakfast?'
'Dinner?'
'Tea?'
'What shampoo do you use?'
'What football team do you support?'
'What do I look like?'

To all of these questions the person being interviewed has to reply 'fish and chips' without smiling or laughing.

Categories

Have two children sitting down facing each other. Give them a category such as something you find in the kitchen, or names of chocolate bars, and so on. Each child takes it in turn to think of something in that category. The one who dries up first or repeats something is out. Choose someone else to take on the champion.

Simon says

Use your own name instead, or invite a child to be 'Simon'.

What am I thinking of?

The leader says "I'm thinking of…" and then chooses a subject such as a letter in the alphabet, or something in this room, a football team, a pop group, a colour, a musical instrument, something you find in a kitchen, something you would see in a church and so on. The children then put their hands up to try to guess what the leader is thinking of. The leader answers only 'yes' or 'no' to each question. Whoever guesses correctly gets a sweet or a point for their team.

Appendix Five

Further resources and training events

Music

Many of the songs that accompany John Hardwick's holiday club and training programmes are available on CD and video. Products include:

High-energy holiday club songs

For details of the *High-energy holiday club songs* CD, see final page. For details of other CDs by John Hardwick, and the *Action Packed Praise* video, also by John Hardwick, contact John via the publishers or directly as follows:

Website: www.johnhardwick.org.uk
Office telephone number: 01223 519489
E-mail johnhardwick36@hotmail.com

Stay legal!

Please remember to tick any songs used during your holiday club or in your weekly church services on your Christian Copyright Licence (CCL) list.

Schools work

John is a member of BRF's *Barnabas Live* team and offers full-day presentations bringing the Bible to life through the creative arts, including music, creative storytelling, puppetry and circus skills. A typical day with John might include:

- A 20-minute assembly with the theme 'Working together and valuing one another'. The assembly includes a juggling talk, song and Bible story told in a dramatic way and is suitable for collective worship across Key Stage 1 and 2.
- A 30-minute class or year group presentation exploring the value of books and the Bible. This includes a Bible story told in a dramatic way, a puppet sketch, song, juggling, unicycling and other circus skills. Ideally, the presentation needs to take place in the school hall or similar space. The material is designed to meet the needs of different year groups across Key Stage 1 and 2 and will be repeated with each year group as required.
- A 'circus skills' workshop suitable for Years 5 and 6. The workshop offers the opportunity for pupils to try their hand at skills such as juggling, plate-spinning, stunt sticks and diabolos. Maximum number per group: 30 children.

To book John for a *Barnabas Live* day, or for further details, contact Eithne (Aina) Nutt at:

BRF
First Floor, Elsfield Hall
15–17 Elsfield Way
Oxford
OX2 8FG

Telephone: 01865 319704
E-mail: eithne.nutt@brf.org.uk

Training events

John Hardwick also offers a range of training events including the following:

- **Training sessions**: A host of ideas with a particular focus on storytelling and music for anyone involved in leading services and events where children are present.
- **Praise parties**: High-energy, fast-moving sessions for primary-aged kids.
- **New songs sessions**: A chance to see John's infectious songs in action.
- **All-age services**: Plenty of variety with a message for everyone.
- **Holiday clubs**: John offers a fun-packed holiday club package including stage-based presentations, songs, Bible narrations and puppetry.

For further information about any of the above products or events, please contact:

John Hardwick
Telephone: 01223 519489/235106
E-mail: johnhardwick36@hotmail.com
Website: www.johnhardwick.org.uk

Puppet suppliers

Children Worldwide

A full range of puppets and other children's resources.

Children Worldwide
Dalesdown
Honeybridge Lane
Dial Post
Horsham
West Sussex
RH13 8NX

Telephone: 01403 711032
Fax: 01403 710716
E-mail: cwide@talk21.com

Hands up for God

People, animal and biblical character puppets plus other related resources and ministry events.

Hands up for God Ministries
Telephone: 01509 415129
E-mail: dennis@dldoyle.freeserve.co.uk
Website: www.handsupforgod.com

Organizations

Children Worldwide has 40 Christian children workers in the UK.
Office: 01403 710712
E-mail: cwide@talk21.com
Website: www.childrenworldwide.co.uk

Scripture Union has over 40 Christian communicators and schools workers in the UK.
Telephone: 01908 856000
E-mail: info@scriptureunion.org.uk
Website: www.scripture.org.uk

Counties has over 40 Christian communicators, many working in schools in the UK.
Telephone: 01373 823013
Fax: 01373 859199
E-mail: counties30@aol.com
Website: http://members.aol.com/counties30

BARNABAS RESOURCES INFORMATION

Please keep me informed about new Barnabas services and resources.

Rev/Dr/Mr/Mrs/Miss _____

Address _____

_____ Post Code _____

Telephone _____ Fax _____

E-mail _____

Do you have responsibilities in any of the following areas?

Sunday School .... ❏	Teacher... ❏
Children's Club .... ❏	*Which age group?*
Which age range?	*Reception* .... ❏
3–5.. ❏	*KS1*... ❏
5–7.. ❏	*KS2*... ❏
7–11 .... ❏	Educational Adviser/Consultant .... ❏
8–12 .... ❏	Church Children's Work Adviser .... ❏

Other (please specify) _____

Please send me

❏   Annual Barnabas Catalogue

Please send me information about

❏   Seasonal resources

❏   Teaching resources for children

❏   Leadership resources

❏   Barnabas Live for schools

❏   Inset training

❏   Training for local church children's leaders

❏   Bible Unplugged events for children

❏   I would like to support Barnabas ministry with a donation

Data Protection Notice

Under the new Data Protection Act legislation BRF must obtain your consent to hold and use information about you. Please sign below to confirm your consent.

BRF will use the information supplied above to fulfil your orders, and to service your requests for further information. The information will be stored both electronically on computer and in a manual filing system until you inform us otherwise. It may be used to inform you of other BRF products, activities and services. BRF will not supply your details to any other companies other than to fulfil orders from BRF.

I confirm my consent to the Data Protection Notice above.

Signed: _____

PLEASE RETURN THIS FORM TO: BRF, FREEPOST (OF758), OXFORD OX2 8YY

First Floor, Elsfield Hall, 15–17 Elsfield Way, Oxford OX2 8FG
Tel: 01865 319700] Fax: 01865 319701] E-mail: enquiries@brf.org.uk
Charity No. 233280] VAT No. GB 238 5574 35

★ ★ ★ ★ ★ ★ ★

OTHER RESOURCES FROM BARNABAS

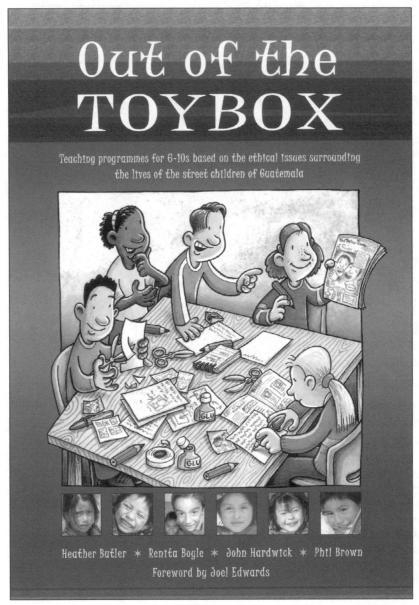

REF 1 84101 239 4, £14.99

The book sets out to explore the ethical issues surrounding the lives of the street children of Guatemala through the work of *The Toybox Charity*, which was founded in 1992 by Duncan and Jenni Dyason. Exploring the issues through three separate but complementary sessions comprising lesson plans, biblical material and a holiday club programme, the material is designed to meet the needs of the teacher and group. Each section stands alone, but also informs and enhances the other two sections. The three sections provide a logical framework, moving from the issues to the Bible and through into action, thus lifting the material off the page and into the lived experience of the child.

Visit the brf website www.brf.org.uk

★ ★ ★ ★ ★ ★ ★

OTHER RESOURCES
FROM BARNABAS

REF 1 84101 253 X, £7.99

We're going on a Jungle Jamboree introduces five key parables from Luke's Gospel, exploring the message behind the story in a contemporary, relevant and fun way. The stories are placed into a jungle setting, taking the child on a journey of adventure on the different routes through life. Each day comprises Bible story narration, serial drama/adventure story, puppet sketches, quick quizzes, jungle games and crafts, action songs with music notation, and differentiated fun sheets. Photocopy permission is included. All the songs are included on the *High-Energy Holiday Club Songs* CD (see next page for details).

High-energy
HOLIDAY CLUB SONGS

Easy-to-sing action songs for Bible-based kids

REF 1 84101 266 1, £8.99 (INCL. VAT)

Look out for John Hardwick's exciting new CD, *High-energy holiday club songs*, especially written and composed to support the material in his two holiday club resource books, *We're going on a Jungle Jamboree* and *Champions!* (both published by BRF).

This CD is an ideal accompaniment to your holiday club programme. It gives you the option to use the full lyrics or just the backing tracks during the holiday club sessions, and provides a lasting memento for the children of their holiday club experience.

High-energy holiday club songs CD is published by BRF, price £8.99.

Includes all the songs and backing tracks from both holiday club programmes.

Available from:
BRF, First Floor, Elsfield Hall,
15–17 Elsfield Way, Oxford OX2 8FG
Telephone: 01865 319700
Fax: 01865 319701
E-mail: enquiries@brf.org.uk

Visit the brf website www.brf.org.uk